*R*evelation
The Road to Overcoming

Charles A. Neal

UNITY® Books

Unity Village, Missouri

To receive a catalog of all Unity publications (books, cassettes, compact discs, and magazines) or to place an order, call the Customer Service Department: (816) 969-2069 or 1-800-669-0282.

Cover design by Jason Rasco

LLC 99 075698
ISBN 0-87159-260-6
Canada BN 13252 9033 RT

Table of Contents

PREFACE

No originality is claimed for the method of interpretation of this work. It is squarely based on the ideas put forward by Charles Fillmore as explained in the Preface to the *Metaphysical Bible Dictionary* published by Unity School of Christianity. The author acknowledges his debt to Unity's co-founder Charles Fillmore, and to numerous other Unity writers and ministers, notably, Eric Butterworth, Winifred Hausmann, J. Sig Paulson, Ed Rabel, and Elizabeth Sand Turner, for their writings and recordings.

The author's purpose in presenting this work is to allow The Revelation to John to be seen for the priceless jewel of inspiration and instruction that it truly is. This Scripture is timeless in its application and an invaluable handbook for assisting the spiritual aspirant when its inner meaning is discovered. All scriptural quotations are taken from the Revised Standard Version of the Bible, unless otherwise identified.

Revelation—Its Purpose

This work is an effort to present the last book of the Bible, The Revelation to John, in a light that is both understandable and helpful, and allow it to be seen from a perspective that will aid all who seek spiritual growth. What is presented here is a metaphysical interpretation based on the belief that humankind is growing and unfolding in a spiritual way and one day will attain recognition of its essential oneness with the one creative Cause of the universe, whom we call God. Our premise is that Jesus Christ knew of His oneness with God, "I and the Father are one" (Jn. 10:30), and He taught that this awareness is also our destiny, "that they may all be one; even as thou, Father, art in me, and I in thee" (Jn. 17:21).

There are other interpretations; in fact, there are at least four ways in which The Revelation to John may be interpreted. These are: (1) *Preterist*, the belief that it was written exclusively for that time and the events have already been fulfilled; (2) *Historical*, the belief that the events described are continuing from the date of the book being written to the end of time; (3) *Futurist*, the belief that the events will take place at the end of time; and (4) *Metaphysical*, the recognition that the message is timeless and, as it is written in a series of symbolic pictures, should be read for its inner meaning disregarding the literal meaning. So vast is God-Mind that all interpretations in their place and context may well be correct.

In this work we have taken the metaphysical approach, and submit it as a possible interpretation based on the belief that the Christ knows well of the problems that face Truth seekers of every age, and so provides a practical handbook to assist spiritual seekers when they strike dry patches in their progress. In the most practical way possible, The Revelation to John was intended to be and is the wayfarer's survival handbook.

In support of this stance, I cannot do better than to quote from a study undertaken by Unity's School for Religious Studies: "It [Revelation] describes the continued unfoldment of a soul *after* an individual has accepted and come into the metaphysical Truth of Jesus Christ. The most important fact to keep in mind when dealing with an interpretation of The Revelation to John is that no matter how fantastic or complex the language of the narrative becomes, it is always talking about a *single individual soul*, which would be any human being who has committed his or her living according to the truths revealed by Jesus Christ."

Apart from a small number of verses that have been taken out of context, when The Revelation to John is compared to the Gospels and Epistles, it has largely been neglected as a subject of study or teaching. But once a new perspective has been attained, The Revelation to John will be seen and valued as a practical source of solace and direction. It will help uncover the reasons for the frustrations of students when they have stumbled, and show them how to regain poise. When seen in this new light, The Revelation to John can be a lifeline for Truth seekers when they are struggling in the deep waters of daily living. In this context it is timeless and not limited to any period—past, present, or future.

The final book of the Bible is a mystery to many. It is probably the least understood of all the Scriptures. It is written in an obscure and highly symbolic apocalyptical style peculiar to Hebrew literature. The word *apocalyptic* has been defined as "the prophetic revelation of that which is hidden." Indeed, for modern readers its meaning is well hidden, for it is hard for the uninitiated to make much sense out of it. Readers are faced with fanciful visions of glorious supernatural beings and outlandish creatures; we are led through horrendous catastrophes, and finally presented with a picture of great peace and serenity.

But apocalyptical literature has, or had, its place. It was written to hearten and inspire the faithful of that day when they were under oppression. The symbolism would be clear to the initiated, but would be meaningless to the rulers not possessing the key to the fantastic pictures presented.

One clear intention of The Revelation to John was to reassure the followers of the Way, who were being persecuted at that time by the full might of the Roman Empire, that the God of Jesus Christ was all-powerful and would triumph in the end.

With the recognition of Christianity as a nationally acceptable religion and the consequent discontinuation of persecution, the question then arose as to the place of The Revelation to John in Christian teaching. There are those who regard it as a book of prophecy. At least two passages are still viewed by some as being prophetic of events as yet unfulfilled. These are: (1) that there will be a final confrontation between the forces of good and evil, to be known as Armageddon (Rev. 16:12-16), and (2) that only 144,000 persons will be "redeemed from the earth" (Rev. 14:1-3); that is, "saved." However, awakened Truth seekers see in The Revelation to John a deeper and more immediate reason for its having been written. It is for them not merely a source of hope and assurance, but a practical "hands-on" aid in times of challenge and possibly wavering faith. In a few words, a survival handbook. But to profit from this we, too, must be put in possession of the key to this understanding.

A prayerful understanding of the design and purpose of the Bible reveals that The Revelation to John is indeed the perfect document to be positioned as its closing book. Briefly summarized, the Bible tells the story of the *generation* of humanity, our *degeneration*, and our progress toward *regeneration*. The Bible opens with the book of Genesis, the book of beginnings, where, in the first chapter, we are told of humanity's generation: "Then God said, 'Let us make man in our image, after our likeness; and let them have dominion . . . .'" So God created man in his own image . . . . And God blessed them, and God said to them . . . 'have dominion' " (Gen. 1:26-28). The second chapter of Genesis tells in allegorical terms of humanity's fall or degeneration. The remainder of the Bible, both Old and New Testaments, tells of humankind's halting efforts toward regeneration, culminating in the advent of Jesus Christ.

By the symbolic act of eating "of the tree of the knowledge of good and evil" (Gen. 2:17), in allegorical form humankind acquired a knowledge of evil (whereas before we had known only good), and so fell from grace into a belief of separation from God. Forgetting that we were truly spiritual beings, one with God, we became hypnotized by the appearances of the material, and so became subject to the evil manifestations of our own minds. Thus we "died" to the awareness of perfection and brought upon ourselves unhappiness, sickness, pain, and inharmony.

In His ministry, Jesus revealed that He knew humankind's true relationship to God. He demonstrated that He, Himself, was essentially spirit, and taught that this is true for all humankind. He said, "I and the Father are one" (Jn. 10:30). A few verses later He added, "Is it not written in your law, 'I said, you are gods'?" (Jn. 10:34) Jesus did not believe in separation, and His ministry was devoted to re-educating humankind to its essentially spiritual nature, and to the truth of His and our oneness with God, All-Good. By this revelation Jesus is our Savior and Way-Shower. He sought to save us from our self-imposed sorrows caused by ignorance, our mistaken belief in separation from God and in the reality of evil. His message was that if we will adhere to His teaching and follow Him by making the necessary changes in our thinking and behavior, we will find freedom, and so ensure that existence on this earthly plane at this time will be rich, enjoyable, and fulfilling. But Jesus emphasized that we have to do the work ourselves. "If any man would come after me, let him deny himself and take up his cross and follow me" (Mt. 16:24).

The Acts of the Apostles and the Epistles contain many stories of persons who endeavored to follow the way Jesus taught. Thousands of lives were changed. These people were in love and at peace with their world. But it is clear that not all the early Christians were successful in this respect. This is true of the faithful of all times, even of this day. We try, but sometimes, oftentimes perhaps, we fail or stumble or, alas, may seem to miss the way completely. So we hit a dry spell, and as a result, we encounter misfortune and unhappiness.

Hence, The Revelation to John! Knowing the fallibility of human nature, God, the Holy Spirit, the Jesus Christ consciousness—call it what we will—in infinite wisdom saw fit to give us the inspired lifeline, The Revelation to John. It shows where we may have fallen short and what we must do to resume what was divinely intended to be a joyous journey on the upward spiritual path. In short, it shows us how to live satisfyingly and healthfully while progressing toward our ultimate goal.

Seen from this standpoint, The Revelation to John is the metaphysical story of the probable experiences of every man and woman. It describes the likely hindrances that stand in our way, and tells us what to do about them. It shows us how to handle almost every conceivable problem and temptation. It shows us where our strengths lie. It describes the prizes that await us as we overcome challenges. It assures us of the certainty of victory as we persist in spite of all our seeming weaknesses and vulnerability. Whatever the odds, whatever the threatened danger, however forboding the appearances, and however powerful the enemy, the sure promise is given: "He who conquers shall have this heritage, and I will be his God and he shall be my son" (Rev. 21:7).

Of course, some may question whether or not it is correct to arbitrarily set aside the belief that The Revelation to John is foretelling a series of events that will take place in the future. The majority of the dramatic and highly colored occurrences and creatures described are clearly not factual. It is therefore unsafe and somewhat illogical to attach unquestioning belief to a few arbitrarily selected vignettes. For this reason, the entire series of events should be viewed as being symbolic, and the surface meaning of them discounted.

It is not our purpose to be dogmatic. These ideas are offered as *only one interpretation* of this mystical book. Others may well be valid. However, we take the position that if spiritual wayfarers of any denomination will accept this approach and guide their thoughts and actions accordingly, they will be enormously helped.

The Comforter

Revelation 1

Now let us turn to our Bibles. For economy of space it is not the intention here to reprint long passages from the Scriptures. Instead, the author recommends that the reader keep a Bible nearby for easy reference. The Revelation to John opens with three verses designed to establish the authority and purpose of the message. In these we are told it is a revelation given by God to Jesus Christ that He might show His servants (followers of the Way) "what must soon take place" (Rev. 1:1). This can be interpreted to be the action of the Comforter whom Jesus promised us in John 14:16, Authorized Version. [In the Revised Standard Version the word *Counselor* is used.] Note the use of the word *must* in

Revelation 1:1. The Comforter has no doubt that the challenges described later would in fact be the lot of the faithful. And "soon" and "the time is near" suggest that the times and need for this guidance are close at hand. We are promised that we will be blessed if we heed the counsel.

Beginning with verse four, John starts to relay the messages. They are addressed to the seven churches. Due to the timelessness of the Jesus Christ teaching, it is unlikely that the word *churches* is intended to refer to the limited congregations as they then existed in Asia Minor. We again emphasize that we are seeking the symbolic and not the literal meaning. The spiritual idea behind the word *church* is a phase of mind dedicated to worship and reverence. It is a particular division of our mental life. The entire book of The Revelation to John is, therefore, a handbook to help guide and direct us in our spiritual seeking.

The message opens (verses four through seven) with a beautiful and loving salutation from the Godhead, glorifying the Christ presence and paying tribute to Jesus, who triumphantly demonstrated the grace and power of that Presence. The speaker is the spirit of God within each of us, and to the degree that we heed or ignore the counsel given, so we are blessed or cast down.

Then the Bible states, " 'I am the Alpha and the Omega,' says the Lord God" (Rev. 1:8). Charles Fillmore tells us: "I AM is God's name in man; it is Jehovah, the indwelling Christ, the true spiritual man whom God made in His image and likeness." I AM, God's spirit in man, the Alpha and the Omega, is the beginning and the end. Our use of the I AM determines our life experience. The I AM is all-embracing; it is all there is; it is all we need; it is the determining factor. The way in which we use statements that include the I AM, whether in thought or verbally, and whether used literally or by implication, decides the nature of our future experience.

John goes on to tell us that these events occurred to him when he was on the island called Patmos. Patmos was then a penal settlement to which he had been banished on account of his witnessing to the teachings of Jesus. In other words, John was in trouble! Now John was a good man. It is no longer believed that this John was "the beloved disciple" of the gospel. He was probably another follower of the Way, but of the same name, and imprisoned for his religious beliefs during the time of the persecution under Emperor Domitian between A.D. 90 and 95. We might well ask ourselves why it was that such a loving individual (implied by the name John) should not by right of consciousness have been allowed to live out his life in peace and harmony. Perhaps the adverse circumstances in which he found himself were the reason that he became the channel for this redemptive message.

Then he tells us how the message was delivered to him. "I was in the Spirit on the Lord's Day" (Rev. 1:10) implies that he was in prayer, in an exalted state of consciousness. He was seeking spiritual answers, when he was startled by a loud voice like a trumpet. The voice did not come from the direction in which he had been looking, but from behind him. This indicates that he had been looking in the wrong direction for the reasons behind the difficulties in which he found himself. Doubtless he had been blaming others, the Romans possibly, for his imprisonment. This reference could be of significance to the spiritual seeker. Perhaps our eyes have been focused on the outer, whereas cause lies within ourselves.

Thus, at the very outset of the work, the Comforter reveals the primary reason for the failure of many of us to find solutions to the challenges we face in life. We have been looking in the wrong direction for answers. We should not look to the outer—to other people, to adverse circumstances, or any material condition—for the reason for our problems. The reason can always be found within ourselves. Consciousness—the totality of our thoughts, feelings, beliefs, prejudices, and preferences—is the one and only cause of every manifestation in our lives. To find reasons for every event, we should first turn within in prayer and seek illumination. Let our first inner turning be to declare: *Let there be light*. Then secondary causes and guidance for remedial action will be revealed.

Then John is instructed to write what he sees in a book, and to send this to the seven churches; that is, to apply it to the various divisions of his spiritual life. John is about to see and hear something of tremendous importance, so important that he should on no account forget it, but write it in a book for permanent reference.

Here it should be noted that for the third time in a short space the number seven is used. Both here and elsewhere in The Revelation to John the number seven signifies completion. It should not be regarded as specifying a precise number or quantity; rather, it refers to sufficiency and completeness. It is an echo of the seven days or stages of creation that resulted in the physical universe being made manifest. So we should not allow ourselves to be hung up on trying to determine which areas of our spiritual life are exclusively referred to, but recognize that there is a need to examine all the areas in our lives that impinge on our spiritual experience.

So John turned and gave his full attention to the speaker. He was dazzled by what he saw, the glorified figure of one like a son of man, resplendently adorned and standing in the midst of seven golden lampstands. This was a vision of the Christ potential in every individual completely illumined. As we read the description of this magnificent Presence in verses twelve through sixteen, it is not recommended that we attempt to arrive at a satisfying interpretation of every last symbol. Rather, we should allow ourselves to be influenced by the overall picture of the glory of the true self when we are not sullied by guilt, selfishness, fear, and the like. Nevertheless, it is of great significance that from his mouth there issued a sharp two-edged sword, an instrument capable of cutting both ways. This indicates the power of the spoken word, particularly when employed in the sense of "I am," whether it be used in the positive or the negative sense.

John is overwhelmed by the appearance of the Christ presence, who identifies Himself as the I AM and informs John that it is our use of statements linked with the I AM that is the key to whether we will live or die and whether our experience here will be heavenly or like a hell on earth. This reiteration of the importance of our correct use of the term I AM is not accidental. No single factor is of greater influence in shaping our lives than being very selective as to what states and conditions we couple with the "I am." To say or think "I am sick, sorry, and unhappy" can only increase the likelihood of our becoming all of those lamentable conditions. Whereas, to repeat often a statement such as "I am healed, whole, well, and joyous" must result in our condition and outlook being improved.

The reference to the seven stars and the seven lampstands again points to the completeness of spiritual self in whom there is every necessary quality. I AM, the Christ, is complete. Nothing more is needed. It is glorious, beautiful, and speaks with authority.

We should be tremendously heartened by this opening vision. It is the annunciation to all humankind. This dazzling Presence is the revelation of the true spiritual nature of us all. This truly is the "imprisoned splendor" locked within each of us, awaiting our discovery and release. This is the truth of humankind. This is the truth of you. This is your destiny!

How to Recapture the Sparkle

Revelation 2:1-7

The second chapter opens with the Christ dictating a message to the angel of the first of the seven churches, the church at Ephesus. While not at first apparent, the Comforter here deals head-on with the primary reason for the difficulties that many seekers of Truth experience. Briefly, it is the sense of discouragement that assails many when they encounter a dry patch in their unfoldment. What once was a joyous journey of spiritual progress and adventure has become a dreary, weary plodding along stony and unrewarding paths.

Metaphysically, the name *Ephesus* contains the ideas of patience, appeal, and fortitude. Reading verses two and three with our inner spiritual eye opened, we understand that Spirit is praising us for our efforts, our prayers and patient work in the silence, our use of denials and affirmations, our having tested other paths and found them wanting, and our final recognition that God is the only answer. However, the all-knowing Christ perceives that all is not well and accurately pinpoints the reason for the malaise. Verse four sternly reads, "But I have this against you, that you have abandoned the love you had at first."

Here the Christ is addressing all seekers on the path who are experiencing a dry spell in their spiritual lives. At one time we knew the elation of the changed life. Our prayers were answered. Life began to take on new meaning. We knew the joy of daily companionship with Spirit. Life was truly an adventure. But now, for some mysterious reason, the magic has evaporated. We continue to observe our prayer times, but these are strangely unproductive. Our use of positive affirmations seems to be valueless. Life has become a burden.

Nevertheless, we are aghast at the accusation, "You have abandoned the love you had at first," or, you no longer love God as you used to. Indignantly we protest, "It is not true that I do not love God as I did. Why, I do love God. I know that God alone can help me." But the Christ is firm and sternly continues, "Remember then from what you have fallen, repent and do the works you did at first. If not, I will come to you and remove your lampstand" (Rev. 2:5). In other words, if we do not change our ways, all the light will go out of our lives.

This is a difficult pill to swallow, but it truly is the reason for the arid periods in our spiritual lives—we are no longer putting God first! We may be sure that whenever we are unhappy, frustrated, or suffering from any disease of mind or body, we are putting other considerations before our love of God. This can be hard to accept, but Spirit helps our understanding by counseling, "Remember then from what you have fallen," or, recall the joyous and exalted state of your mind when you first came into Truth. In those magic days you were uplifted and confident. You had glimpsed the tremendous possibilities of a new life resulting from a changed way of thinking. No matter what befell, you were filled with burning faith. You did not yet demonstrate faith on every level, but seeming miracles happened. Recall your affirmations ringing with assurance: *I am healed. I am whole. I am well. I live, move, and have my being in the opulence of God.* You were uplifted. Get back to that state of mind. Recapture your first enthusiasm.

The key to this passage lies in a proper understanding of what it takes to love God. God is life, and life is good. In Truth, all life experience is good, however harsh an isolated incident may appear. This is so because every individual life is a learning process, and we have caused or invited every event as the necessary next step in our spiritual growth. We may have an accident, be bereaved, or incur a loss, and we label these events evil. But Jesus instructed us not to resist evil, to have a single eye, which implies that we see only the good. Our part then is to know that there is a blessing in every occurrence. We should, for example, call an accident good and take advantage of the enforced rest. When bereaved, let us release our loved ones, knowing they have fulfilled their earthly assignment and are still in God's care, preparing themselves for their next experience. Meanwhile, we should remind ourselves that life is for living fully in the here and now.

So it is with every seeming disappointment and every delayed answer to prayer. There is a reason for it. The answer lies in trusting

God, and above all, loving God enough to know this present situation is for our highest good. In this way we can recapture the joy and excitement that we had when we first realized the truth that we are not just human beings but spiritual beings embodying the Christ potential. Life is good now, and the only factor that prevents us from enjoying it deeply is our approach to it, our attitude to life.

Continuing with our Scripture, Spirit then commends us for hating the work of the Nicolaitans. The Nicolaitans had introduced pagan practices into worship and so debased it. We become pagans when we think negatively, so our part is to resolve always to think in a positive, constructive manner. We are commended for our attempts to remain optimistic and positive.

Then the loving Spirit gives us the sure promise, "To him who conquers I will grant to eat of the tree of life, which is in the paradise of God" (Rev. 2:7). Who are we to conquer? Why, ourselves, of course—our own moodiness, our impatience, our sense of disappointment, our demand for instant gratification. "To eat of the tree of life" means to know that every experience feeds us; that we can gain spiritual nourishment and strength from every happening, both from seeming adversity and from everything that we call fortunate. Whatever happens, if we will take every event in our stride and declare that it is only good, good it will prove to be.

A young mother had to take her small daughter into a large city several times a week by means of a commuter train, a journey that lasted the best part of two hours. She had hoped that this would be a time in which she could continue her studies, but the restlessness of the child effectively prevented this. The mother would try to read, but the child would tug on her for attention and climb on her lap. She would refuse to settle down, pestering her mother with questions about the passing scene, and wriggling around, making study quite impossible. The mother would become increasingly irritated with the child, and as her patience was exhausted she would snappily correct the child. The child would respond by crying and making a nuisance of herself to other passengers. The mother began to dread the journeys, and felt humiliated and embarrassed at her inability to control the child.

One day in her prayer time she came to the realization that she should find good in every event in her life. There must be some good purpose in having to make these journeys. There must be good for the child and herself. She loved her daughter and decided to demonstrate that love by devoting herself to her child, and leaving it to God to provide the right opportunities for her studies. Accordingly, when they were next required to travel she was prepared with storybooks. Once they boarded the train she gave herself entirely to meeting her daughter's needs. She answered the child's questions, then read from the storybooks. Before very long, the child became drowsy and shortly was fast asleep. The mother was able to spend the rest of the trip concentrating on her studies, and both arrived fresh and happy at their destination. This pattern became a habit and both enjoyed the trips into the city.

This is a practical application of the principle of what truly loving God entails. It involves appreciating every event that we face in life and using it to good advantage. By changing her attitude and unselfishly seeking to put her child's need before her own, my friend was able to convert what at first appeared to be a negative situation into a time of profit and joy. She was enabled to recapture the sparkle that was divinely intended to grace our journey on the spiritual path.

The Prosperity Secret

Revelation 2:8-11

Framed in a message to the angel of the church in Smyrna, found in Revelation 2:8-11, "the first and the last, who died and came to life," that is, the Christ, now directs our attention to the true source of prosperity. Metaphysically the word *Smyrna* means "substance." It is derived from Greek and Hebrew roots which include the ideas of flowing, distilling, and being spirituous. In the Greek, Smyrna means "myrrh" (one of the three rich gifts presented by the Magi to the infant Jesus). So this letter is a veiled instruction to that area of our spiritual observance that controls the flow of substance and its distillation into our lives and experiences to meet our daily needs. It condemns our misuse of substance and tells us the secret of true prosperity.

Substance is one of the ideas of Divine Mind. It is the invisible mind-essence of God out of which everything is made. It is formless, invisible, unlimited, and everywhere equally present. We are told in Genesis that in the beginning, when the universe was without form, God-Mind moved on itself. In other words, the active element of Divine Mind, the Logos, moved on its passive element, substance, and said, "Let there be," and out of this substance the universe came into manifestation. This substance is still present, all around, permeating, penetrating, and interpenetrating us. Substance is infinitely responsive to the mind of humankind, which was given dominion. Out of this we construct our life experience. When we shape a thought, an invisible mold is made into which is poured the substance of our thinking. This eventually reproduces outer events and circumstances that are in accord with those thoughts, modified, of course, by all our other thoughts.

This process is illustrated by the story of the small boy who prayed, in effect: "Father-God, please send me a pony. I want a pony very much. But I realize Mother does not

want me to have one, and I also know that
Father does not want to build a stable, and
the chances are he cannot afford a pony. Then
there's the question of who will clean up after
the pony. So, Father, I guess it's hopeless;
but I would still like a pony."

Many of us pray in a similar manner. We
ask for some desired object or event, but our
minds are full of all the many difficulties that
lie in the path of the request being granted.
All these conflicting thoughts have their effect in shaping the flow of substance into our
lives as manifestations. This principle ac-
counts for the many often contradictory experiences that some of us encounter. Substance is the true and only source of all things
and events, and its flow is controlled by our
consciousness. Truly, we are all self-made individuals, and by our thinking we determine
whether we are to be congratulated or to
receive commiseration!

Here the Christ is saying to that part of our
spiritual makeup that handles and shapes
substance, "I know your tribulation and your
poverty (but you are rich) and the slander of
those who say that they are Jews and are not,
but are a synagogue of Satan" (Rev. 2:9). Remember, the Bible was written by Jewish
people. The word *Jews* in this passage refers

to those who are spiritually minded, those who are consciously seeking God and Truth. Thus, the Christ is telling us that if we do not feel prospered, it is because we only think we are seeking in Truth the answer to our seeming lack, when in fact we are not truly in a spiritual consciousness. The truth is we are harboring doubts, fears, and negative thoughts, and praying in the manner of the small boy in the story. We think we are praying for a certain outcome, but at the same time we are pouring a stream of negation into the mold that must manifest as our experience. So the Comforter is saying to us in this somewhat involved fashion, "Get rid of these contradictory concepts, for so long as you hold them, you are not putting God first."

Genuine truth seekers know that life experience is determined by consciousness; this includes awareness of God as being our one and only source and resource. We know that we are one with God and that as we unfailingly work with the universal laws of love, compassion, and forgiveness, so will all our needs be unfailingly and opulently met. But at the same time we must ensure that we are correctly using and shaping substance by our positive and unselfish attitudes.

This involves a lively and unmistakable appreciation that indeed God is our only source, and that all other seeming sources are but channels. The temptation to confuse a channel with the source is a very subtle one, and many fall into this error. By so doing, they reveal themselves as materialistic and unwittingly affiliate themselves with a "synagogue of Satan." It is essential that we correctly identify the various avenues through which our supply comes to us for what they are, namely, channels only. Salary, wages, pensions, alimony, dividends, royalties, rents, or whatever, are but channels and should be recognized as such. God substance is our one and only source. Any one or more of the channels may be closed, but our security is assured if our mental treatment of substance is correct, for as the Comforter says parenthetically, we are rich!

We can apply a simple test to see whether or not we are in a spiritual or material consciousness. If we believe that any of the following statements are true, then we are in a material consciousness:

"To be secure, I must have a lot of money and many possessions."

"Somebody else can take my good away from me."

"I can profit by taking something that belongs to another."

"I will be poorer if one of my channels is closed to me."

"I must look after number one, for no one else will."

All these are widely held beliefs, but are demonstrably false. This kind of thinking governs the marketplace and doubtless has made many people rich. But where riches have been obtained by use of this kind of philosophy they have proved to be impermanent and have produced unhappiness.

It was reported in the once widely read Billy Rose syndicated column that in 1923, a meeting was held at the Edgewater Beach Hotel in Chicago at which nine of the world's greatest financiers were present. They were Charles Schwab, president of the world's largest steel company; Samuel Insul, president of the largest utility company; Arthur Cotton, wheat speculator; Richard Whitney, president of the New York Stock Exchange; Albert Fall, member of the cabinet; Ivar Krugar, head of the world's greatest monopoly; Jesse Livermore, prominent "bear" of Wall Street; Leon Fraser, president, Bank of International Settlement; and Howard Hopson, president of the world's largest gas company. It was stated that these men gathered to put together a deal to make them all richer. Twenty-five years later, Charles Schwab had died a bankrupt; Samuel Insul died penniless and a fugitive from justice; Arthur Cotton died insolvent; Richard Whitney and Albert Fall both went to jail; Ivar Krugar, Leon Fraser, and Howard Hopson all committed suicide. This is not meant to condemn riches but to comment on the way in which they are obtained. Contrast these men with Andrew Carnegie, a great philanthropist who gave millions to charity. He died rich, leaving $125 million in a charitable foundation that has proved to be a blessing to countless persons.

It is of the utmost importance that we always maintain a spiritual attitude to riches and supply and that we avoid falling into the trap of materialism. The truth is that no one can take your good away from you if it is truly yours by right of consciousness. Equally, no one can permanently add to his store if he takes that which belongs to another. The thief, for example, always operates from the standpoint of lack. He believes there is not enough to go around, and that the only way in which his needs can be met is to take that which belongs to another. Operating from the standpoint of lack, he must inevitably remain in a state of insufficiency because his consciousness is one of lack and limitation. This same principle is involved wherever a person seeks to make a profit by some sharp practice, by cutting quality, or by seeking only to make a bargain. The splendid truth is that there is no lack or limitation in God, and if we will cultivate our sense of oneness with God, we will not experience limitation. But if our actions are governed by a belief in limitation, then limitation must have its way with us. We decide.

Verse ten warns that if we follow the path of blatant self-interest, we will be imprisoned by our own sense of limitation. But take heart, for the verse continues, "Be faithful unto death, and I will give you the crown of life." Be faithful to God until this self-imposed condition of poverty comes to an end when you realize that you truly rule your own life.

In this awareness, we are now better equipped to understand the concluding statement, "He who has an ear, let him hear what the Spirit says to the churches. He who conquers shall not be hurt by the second death" (Rev. 2:11). What is the "second death"? For that matter, what is the "first" death? One can interpret the first death as occurring when we kill off the little ego and recognize our responsibility to others. That is, when we begin to share, to give unselfishly to our church or charities, without fearing that every gift will diminish our supply; when we begin to see ourselves as stewards of supply rather than owners; when we kill off the last remnants of the belief that God's universe can be limited in any way.

The "second death," then, would refer to the passing of any existing condition, the occurrence of any apparent loss. Paraphrased, this last verse says: Understand the necessity of rightly using your own mind. Look to God as your one source, knowing that in truth you are rich, and you will have no reason to fear any possible loss or change of circumstances in the future.

Highway or Byway?

Revelation 2:12-17

Our study brings us to verses twelve through seventeen of the second chapter. The Christ presence now confronts the tendency of followers of the Way in the first century, and students of Unity and New Thought in this or any age, to continue their intellectual search for Truth on paths that are not always profitable. The early Christians had broken the bonds of their rigid beliefs in Judaism or Hellenism and had embraced a new, freeing religion. Similarly, today, Unity and other New Thought students have found freedom in Truth principles. Their very openness of mind leads them to continue their search and frequently to become interested in teachings that are peripheral, and which do not aid them in their search for the rich and full life. These teachings may not of themselves be harmful, but they are detours off the highway to Truth. They become meanderings along byways, and usually end up as dead ends. This produces frustration and disappointment.

Outwardly, the message is addressed to the angel of the church of *Pergamum*, a Greek name meaning "strongly united, closely knit, a citadel." Its metaphysical meaning is the intellectual consciousness. The Christ tells us that it is here, in the intellect, that Satan reigns. Satan stands for the adversary— negative beliefs—and of course, these are held in mind. The message is therefore aimed at our thinking and reasoning processes that are contrary to pure Truth.

However, our minds are not wholly to be deprecated, for they are praised for their faith, even to the point of willingness to die for strongly held beliefs. We are commended for standing firm even to the point of martyrdom.

Spirit continues, "But I have a few things against you: you have some there who hold to the teaching of Balaam . . . that they might eat food sacrificed to idols and practice immorality. So you have some who hold to the teaching of the Nicolaitans. Repent then.''

There are many ways in which we can, in the figurative sense, hold to the teachings of Balaam or the Nicolaitans, and eat food sacrificed to idols. They concern a tendency to become caught up in outer observances to the neglect of consistently seeking Truth in mind. The basic tenet of Truth is: *We are spiritual beings, made in the image after the likeness of God, one with God by virtue of the I AM, the Christ presence within us. God-Mind is our one source and resource.* This is all we need to know and to practice. However, in our seeking it is possible to be attracted by certain outer practices and beliefs that seem to increase our spirituality, but which in fact are merely exercises in futility. It should be emphasized that none of the practices or beliefs about to be cited are evil or harmful in themselves, but they are not helpful because they do not aid spiritual seekers in the attainment of their goal, namely, the awareness and expression of Christ consciousness. Pilgrims may become so caught up in observing these outer practices that they lose sight of their objective.

The list of such bypaths is endless, and we will only briefly examine some. There are those who believe that a certain diet (any one of many) or certain body positions or methods of breathing are essential. These may, indeed, be beneficial to one's health, but belief that they will increase spirituality is worshiping a false god. There are some who believe that spiritualism or psychism are evidences of spirituality. These may be helpful in that they assist some to understand something of the continuity of life, but they are not of themselves essential. It is better that we should regularly practice prayer and meditation and come into the awareness of the inner Presence for ourselves than go to mediums.

Some fall into the trap of placing on a pedestal certain gurus, earthly teachers, healers, ministers, ascended masters, and the like, believing they have some special relationship with the Deity. Others place great credence in channeled writings, believing that these are the product of some entity of high spiritual eminence. Again, these beliefs may indeed be valid, but we question whether they assist the pilgrim in spiritual growth. We are on this plane to develop our own mastery, and we are not helped by relying on intermediaries and giving them special authority. Others relinquish self-dominion by placing undue credence on the position of the stars at the time of their birth. The position of heavenly bodies may or may not have some influence, but it is better to regard this as referring only to tendencies, rather than vesting in them an ironclad statement as to the future. We are not pawns but spiritual beings with the freedom to evolve as we elect.

A further area is the interest that some display in who or what they may have been in some past life. The twin doctrines of reincarnation and karma are to many an acceptable explanation of the continuity of life as an alternative to the traditional belief in one life and heaven or hell after death. Charles Fillmore called it "the doctrine of the second chance." However, it is important that we should live one life at a time. We have no need to inquire into the past, for all the information we need to live this life satisfactorily exists in our present experience. We are daily faced with challenges of one sort or another, and these embody all that we need to know about our reason for being on this earth plane at this time. The lessons that we have to learn are contained in the circumstances and relationships that are ours now. We do not need to seek information about previous lives in order to account for some of the events that face us today. Others, on learning of something that is supposed to be the cause of a present challenge, shrug and say, "Well, there's nothing I can do about it; it's my karma!" But as Emmet Fox wrote, "Christ is Lord of Karma," implying, there is nothing in this or any previous life that cannot be overcome by turning within to the Christ.

Any or all of these and many other beguiling teachings can absorb a great deal of spiritual and mental energy. They may be interesting, but none of them will take us farther along the spiritual path. They are but byways, and we have consumed time in following them when we would have been better continuing our journey along the highway of Truth.

The list of errors spoken by Spirit to the church included reference to immorality. The Authorized King James Version of the Bible renders this passage as: "to commit fornication" (Rev. 2:14). Although the reference is not to sexuality, it does help us understand. The fornicator transfers his error to another. The passage is speaking out against teaching these as being *true steps* to spirituality. There is nothing wrong with them as areas of interest, but they should not be regarded as steps to spiritual growth.

Some time ago an individual came to see me who had been visiting a local "medium counselor" from whom she had been seeking "spiritual" guidance. The medium had informed her that she would shortly be experiencing bad luck, because an enemy had cast a spell on her. For cash, the medium would remove the spell, but it would take time—and regular contributions. At this time the lady had already parted with $400 and now the medium requested another $1,000.

My visitor asked, "What do you think of spiritualist mediums?" I responded by asking what she thought of them. She stated she did not know what to think, but that she had a feeling her bad luck had already started, for she was $400 out of pocket, and there was no end in sight. I agreed. This lady was wandering along what could be a very expensive byway. She was worshiping a false god!

In prayer, I endeavored to bring her back to the highway, to recognize the one indwelling Presence and Power, God the good, within her. We prayed together, recognizing the one indwelling Presence. We prayed for freedom from any belief in spells and in luck, whether good or bad. We rested in the silence, during which time I visualized her back on the highway. She left, promising to think over what I had said.

I do not know the outcome of her session

with me, but I am confident that if she has re-mained on the byway and returned to her spiritualist medium, then the prediction of bad luck will certainly be fulfilled. On the other hand, if she has returned to the high-way, she will eventually find her way to the rich and fulfilling life.

The promise is given to those who hear and repent (that is, change their way of thinking), "To him who conquers I will give some of the hidden manna, and I will give him a white stone, with a new name written on the stone which no one knows except him who receives it" (Rev. 2:17). Of all the rich promises given to us in the Bible, this surely must be one of the most wonderful. The "hidden manna" im-plies nourishment and joy from a hidden source, the very spirit of God indwelling. This is food for the soul that surpasses anything that we have known hitherto. There will be a never-ceasing flow of manifest good in that life. Spirit will indeed seem to "open the win-dows of heaven" (Mal. 3:10) and pour forth a series of rich blessings.

Then, the promise of the white stone with a new name. When using the I AM, we may be both announcing our name and describing our condition. Before, we may well have been holding such concepts as: I am sick, unwell, poor, unhappy, dissatisfied, and frustrated. Now, however, because of the welling up from the secret source within, we have a new concept of ourselves and we will be able to refer to ourselves in terms that only we know, such as: I am richly blessed; I am thankful; I am joyous; I am healed; I am whole and well; I am the beloved child of a rich and opulent Father; I am the beloved child of God in whom He is well pleased. Thus we grow into a new and richer concept of who we truly are. It is written on the white stone of our purified consciousness. We begin to glimpse something of the magnificence of the I AM. This is not a promise that may or may not be fulfilled; it describes the sure and inevitable condition that must invariably follow our patient adherence to Truth as we persist on the highway and resist the siren songs that emanate seductively from the byways of life.

Zeal for Thy House

Revelation 2:18-29

The indwelling Christ now turns to another aspect of the religious life that has bedeviled Christians throughout the ages. It probably is a human tendency that existed before the Christian era and is likely always to be a matter to be reckoned with; namely, misplaced zeal. As we saw in the lesson spoken to the church at Ephesus, enthusiasm for our faith is essential. However, there can be times when zeal for our beliefs can get out of hand and become a negative factor. The Christ deals with this tendency in His message to the angel of the church at Thyatira as it is recorded in the second chapter of The Revelation to John, verse nineteen to the end.

The passage begins: "I know your works,

your love and faith and service and patient endurance, and that your latter works exceed the first" (Rev. 2:19). The metaphysical meaning of *Thyatira* is: "rushing headlong," "burning incense," or "zeal in religious matters." In the opening words, the follower of the Way is praised for his accomplishments, his faith and endurance, and the fact that his later accomplishments exceed his earlier ones. However, Spirit then attacks the listener for tolerating Jezebel (verse twenty). [This Jezebel is a symbolic name. It is not to be taken literally as the wife of Ahab.] The name *Jezebel* means "licentious, emotionally uncontrolled." She is the daughter of Ethbaal, the King of Sidon. The word *Ethbaal* means "given over to materiality" and the word *Sidon* stands for great increase of ideas in the animal level of thinking. We are told, "Jezebel, who calls herself a prophetess and is teaching and beguiling my servants . . . " (Rev. 2:20). In other words, the subject has assumed the mantle of authority on religious matters and his enthusiasm has gotten out of hand as he seeks to impose his views on others. Further, the subject's enthusiasm is no longer purely spiritual in its seeking but has taken on material aspects.

It is tempting to digress at this point and

consider how appropriately this injunction applies to the Christian church throughout the centuries. Scarcely had the church emerged from the persecutions of secular rulers when it seems that a measure of materiality crept in. Enormous houses of worship were built, the ruling heirarchy clothed themselves in the garments of authority, intolerance was rife, giving rise to holy wars and the Inquisition, accompanied by torture and burnings. All of this occurred in the name of religion, but the church seemed to forget the message of its founder whose teachings were love, tolerance, and forgiveness. Christianity had given way to "churchianity." The universal church itself may well have been the object of the message to Thyatira.

However, in this work we are concerned primarily with the application of the message to the individual soul who has committed himself or herself to living the Christ life. Let there be no mistake—there are many occasions when the individual has need to heed this message. We can become emotionally and enthusiastically attached to some material or physical aspect of our religion at the expense of the deep, inner personal change that is so necessary, yet apparently harder to attain. Eric Butterworth puts it very well:

"Men of all time have deluded themselves with the belief that outward acts that seem so easy can be made to take the place of interior changes of thought and feeling which seem to be more difficult" (*Discover the Power Within You*; Harper & Row, New York).

One area which is a very subtle one concerns the tendency of some people to become so zealous about their church that they neglect their homes, their families, and their normal social obligations. Above all, Truth should be a uniting factor, not a divisive element. Our religion should make us better husbands, wives, parents, children, or neighbors. It is a teaching of love and understanding. Occasionally, an individual becomes so "spiritual" that he or she refuses normal physical intimacy with the spouse, thus imposing this concept of spiritual purity on his or her mate. Every individual has the spiritual obligation to carry out the social responsibilities implied in the marriage contract. Paul is emphatic on this point and states that individuals should only withhold themselves by mutual consent. There are clear dangers to one-sided celibacy. These are, first, that the neglected mate may well seek the arms of another, and second, that the abstainer may

possibly yield to the temptation of becoming unfaithful with another "highly spiritual" individual. Of course, in the eyes of the
couple this is regarded as a "spiritual" union,
but it is nonetheless infidelity, and the spiritual seeker has, in fact, experienced a setback.

A second area of misplaced zeal is the temptation to thrust one's newly found beliefs on
others in his circle. After years of wandering
in the spiritual wilderness, the seeker has
found a way that works and, oh, how glorious
it is! Having discovered that answers to
many of life's problems can be found by turning within to the Christ, this is clearly the
answer also for one's wife, husband, parents,
children, and others. Enthusiastically the
convert preaches to all who will listen, but
alas, to his astonishment few are interested.
How blind can they be? He may well have forgotten that he, himself, was unable to embrace this revolutionary way of thinking until
he was ready to accept it. Jesus had warned
us against casting pearls before swine, and in
the figurative sense this is being done. Family and friends have to travel their own paths
and will be unprepared to accept a new way of
thinking and living until they, too, have
seemingly exhausted every other route. At all

times we should remember that we cannot
live the lives of our loved ones for them. Just
as we had to take every painful step on our
own road, so our loved ones must be free to go
their own way.

There are, however, two steps we can take.
One, by all means hand them literature that
we believe will be helpful to them, and possibly invite them to attend a class or service.
This should be done without pressure. We
must lovingly release others to the care and
keeping of their own indwelling Christ. Two,
our emphasis should always be on making
Truth work in our own lives. Demonstrate
that this Truth way of thinking brings with it
new health, joy, prosperity, and harmony in
relationships. Seek to become so changed
that others will notice the difference and long
to have it for themselves. When you are easier to live with, they will want to know the
secret.

Further evidence that we have allowed Jezebel to influence us is intolerance of the religions of others. There is a golden thread of
Truth running through all religions. Every
person is drawn by consciousness to that set
of beliefs that is right for him or her at that
stage of spiritual development. Even though
someone's beliefs may appear to be based on

outdated and limited teachings—even on superstition—one is in one's right place until one's own indwelling Spirit prompts one to make a change. Again, the best course in such conditions is to become a radiant, loving example of the joyous influence of Truth, and be sure that our enthusiasm is constantly directed to developing more and more of our own Christ expression.

The influence of Jezebel may also be evidenced in our lives by our avidly seeking demonstrations at the expense of genuine spiritual growth. It is not unusual that our first touch with Truth was to meet a need in our own experience, but the answer to that problem came as we attained a new and deeper understanding of our relationship to the Christ indwelling. Changes in the outer always come as a result of prior changes in consciousness. Good health, harmonious relationships, and ample supply to meet all our needs are part of the loving provision of the Creator for us, but these come as the result of recognition of our oneness with God and not when sought as ends in themselves. As our beloved Teacher and Way-Shower told us, "But seek first his kingdom and his righteousness, and all these things shall be yours as well" (Mt. 6:33).

The foregoing are examples of ways in which misplaced zeal may threaten our spiritual life. To summarize, they are to:

● Place too much emphasis on the outer trappings of religion.

● Neglect home responsibilities in the name of religion.

● Endeavor to thrust our religious beliefs on others.

● Be critical or intolerant of the religion of others.

● Avidly seek material demonstrations before spiritual growth.

The Revelation to John states that those who are beguiled by Jezebel into engaging in these or any similar excesses in the name of religion will be thrown into great tribulation, and the children of the union will die. This is not an idle threat but is a statement of immutable law. Although it is not to be taken literally that one's human children will die, trouble must inevitably follow any such attempts to trample on the spiritual freedoms of others, possibly in the form of alienation or a breakdown in relationships, and the perpetrator will experience frustration and unhappiness. Further, the efforts will prove fruitless and produce nothing of lasting good, for "I will strike her children dead" (Rev. 2:23).

What follows is the heartening promise of reassurance for those who are able to resist the temptation to thrust their religious beliefs onto others: "I will give him power over the nations, and he shall rule them with a rod of iron . . . and I will give him the morning star" (Rev. 2:26-28). Just as we give freedom to others, so we experience freedom. This is the ability to control our own thoughts and feelings. As we resist the temptation to interfere in the lives of others, so we build within ourselves the power to rule our own emotions, and the light of divine guidance, like that of the morning star, will shine in our minds to guide and direct us into ways of joy and peace. As we are tolerant of the beliefs of others, so we are free from intolerance and from interference from the outer.

We Are More Than We Know

Revelation 3:1-6

Hidden in the message to the angel of the church in Sardis is the spiritual reason for the feeling of helplessness that pervades so many people, and what steps should be taken to heal this condition. We find it in the third chapter of The Revelation to John, verses one through six. The statement is introduced as being: "The words of him who has the seven spirits of God and the seven stars." Hence, we understand this message emanates from the Source and that this Source is completely wise and illumined in every respect. It implies the allness of God—Omniscience, Omnipotence, and Omnipresence.

The word *Sardis* has an interesting metaphysical meaning. It means "precious gem;

prince of joy; inner center of individual power, dominion, and authority." Freely translated, this means that each of us has an inner center of power, dominion, and authority that is a precious gem, and by virtue of ownership we become princes or princesses of joy. This precious gem is our often unrealized inner power to take dominion over our own lives. It is our use of this inner power that is under consideration.

There is a fascinating true story out of history that illustrates the principle. Alvar Núñez Cabeza de Vaca was second-in-command of an expedition of some six hundred men who sailed in three ships from Spain to the Western world in 1527. The expedition was wrecked in a hurricane off the coast of Texas, and Cabeza de Vaca and six other men were the only survivors. Nearly dead, they crawled ashore where they were greeted by Indians who fed and cared for them. Noting the lighter skins of the Spaniards, and coupled with the fact that they had come from the East, the Indians assumed they were gods and implored them to heal their sick, of whom there were many. Cabeza de Vaca and his men were aghast at the request, and through the use of signs made it clear that they were only humans with no special powers. The Indians were angered by the refusal and imprisoned the Spaniards in a stockade, without food, and left them there to die. Finally, desperately hungry and feeling they had nothing to lose, Cabeza and his men agreed to make what they thought would be an abortive attempt at healing the sick Indians. They were released to move among the sick natives. Although only laymen, they prayed earnestly and made the sign of the cross over the invalids. To their complete astonishment, the Indians were healed. Months later, after they had reached a Spanish settlement, Cabeza wrote to the King of Spain, saying in effect, "Your Majesty, we seemingly ordinary men are more than we know. We have abdicated our powers to the priests and physicians, but we have become aware that there is within us power we do not suspect. We are more than we know!" It is our forgetting this stark but simple Truth that prompts this present message in The Revelation to John.

The description of the condition of the subject's soul is brutally direct: "I know your works; you have the name of being alive, and you are dead" (Rev. 3:1). As Truth students we understand that we have been made in the image of the Creator, with dominion, and so have the power to form the conditions of our own lives. It was intended that we should exert this power to produce lives that will be full and satisfying as we progress on our spiritual way. But, we "have the name of being alive, and [you] are dead." We have the name of being children of God with dominion, but we have misused our inherent power to claim dominion over the conditions of our own lives.

The reasons for this are several. First, traditional religion has not taught us of the existence of this power. To the contrary, we have been taught that our very nature is depraved and our salvation is made possible only by outside intervention. We have been conditioned to believe that we are pawns of fate, at the mercy of hostile elements in our world, miserable sinners at best. Despite our new knowledge that we are born to have dominion, the old beliefs are difficult to eradicate. There is often an uneasy feeling that it is somewhat blasphemous to take upon ourselves the powers that we have been taught to believe inhere in God alone.

Then there is the mistaken belief that we should not bother God with trifles, and we should only call on our inner powers in matters of great concern. To the contrary, we should take steps to exercise at every conceivable opportunity the powers that have been given to us. Truly, it should become "first nature" to take spiritual control of every event in life. We should declare divine order in every situation; we should speak the word to manifest healing, prosperity, and order and harmony in every condition. In every health or financial challenge, the first step should be the inner turning for divine direction. We are here to demonstrate our complete oneness with God, and this can only come by habitual thinking and practice of that oneness.

Spirit says, "Awake, and strengthen what remains and is on the point of death" (Rev. 3:2). If we do not arouse ourselves to the importance of the right use of the power within us, it will die. We will lose the ability to control our destiny; we will, indeed, become pawns. Then Spirit states, "I have not found your works perfect . . . " (Rev. 3:2), or, we have used the power, but wrongly. The negative side of this principle is demonstrated when we use the power of thought or of the spoken word to produce misfortune in our experience. We do this every time we think or speak negatively or pessimistically. It is vital to watch every use of the I AM in our speech and thought. Thoughts or statements such as "I am poor, sick, and unhappy" invite like experiences and unhappiness.

Then Spirit sternly warns, "If you will not awake, I will come like a thief . . . " (Rev. 3:3), implying that our ability to use the precious gem positively will be taken from us. It resolves into a matter of continuing to watch attitudes. These are formed by constant use. The optimistic person who speaks approvingly of conditions and expectations is correctly using the power entrusted to him or her, while the pessimistic individual will most certainly invite misfortune by the misuse of mind.

However, we are not entirely lost, for Spirit says, "You have still a few . . . who have not soiled their garments; and they shall walk with me in white, for they are worthy" (Rev. 3:4). Paraphrased, there are still some areas where we have not abdicated our powers, and as we continue to use our power in those areas, we will have a sense of purity and worthiness.

Then Spirit tells us that as we change our way of thinking and overcome our failure to use the inner power in every area of our lives, so we will be clad in white garments; that is, we will enjoy a sense of purity and worthiness. And Spirit goes on, "I will not blot his name out of the book of life" (Rev. 3:5). While we were engulfed in the sense of helplessness and impotence, we were in essence "blotted out of the book of life," for life had neither meaning nor purpose for us. Now comes the promise that the sense of meaninglessness and of purposelessness will be removed, and new zest and joy for life will be experienced. For the sublime promise is given: "I will confess his name before my Father and before his angels" (Rev. 3:5). This means that as we enjoy the elation of constant, conscious communication with the Father, we will receive wonderful, inspiring ideas.

It is never too late nor inappropriate for us to ask ourselves whether or not we have felt that to some degree we have been blotted out of the book of life. The remedy lies as close as a change in attitude. A woman who had been a Unity member for twenty years came to me for counsel. She did not attend the church I served, but lived in a city some forty miles away and was a regular listener to my radio program. She complained of feeling unwell and of being neglected by her children who lived in a northern state. Her physician could find nothing organically wrong and suggested that she enter the hospital for tests.

This she dreaded, yet she was afraid to ignore the advice. What should she do?

It seemed that she had become increasingly reclusive since the death of her husband some ten years before. None of her friends came to see her. She prayed only intermittently, and did not meditate. She was a classic case of one who had "the name of being alive, but was dead." She said she was Unity, but was not. She may have glimpsed the true Jesus Christ message that Unity teaches, but she had not grasped it. She was still awaiting an outside Savior in some form to save her, whereas her salvation could come only from within. The inner Christ was saying: "Awake, and strengthen what remains and is on the point of death .... Repent" (Rev. 3:2-3). Begin to think in a new, triumphant, and optimistic way.

As her counselor I was privately sure that if she entered the hospital for tests she would be so full of tension that she would psychosomatically produce some physical manifestation that would call for removal, resulting in the surgery she feared. I did not counsel her not to enter the hospital. That had to be her own decision. But I did advise her to recognize the Christ power within her and to begin using her mind in a positive and faith-filled way. Her need was not so much for tests as for a bright, new, joyous attitude toward life.

We prayed together, spending time resting in a relaxed silence after having spoken the word that her inner Guide would show her what course to take. When we had finished, she sat smiling. She said that she had become very relaxed, and the uncomfortable, stifled feeling in her abdomen had disappeared. Then she said that she had received two clear and distinct ideas. One was that now that the pain had gone, she should not go to the hospital; and the second was that she should attend a social function that was taking place in her mobile home park that evening.

She called me about six months later, sounding very happy. She had joined the social activities at her park and had made new friends. One of her friends was regularly visited by a brother who was a widower, and they had started dating. She was now about to be married and would be moving away, and had called to say "Thank you and good-bye." This lady obtained a new lease on what we trust would be a joyous and satisfying way of living by turning within and using the guidance and the power of the indwelling Christ. She had powers within her that she did not suspect. She was more than she knew!

Philadelphia refers to the necessity for increased expression of love on the human
level.

The sender of this message describes Himself as "the holy one, the true one, who has
the key of David, who opens and no one shall
shut." This introduction indicates the importance of the message that follows, for it is
remitted by Him who is "holy" and "true"
(the Godhead) and also "has the key of
David." David represents for us an elevated
expression of human love. From his line, the
house of David, sprang Jesus, who epitomized Christ love. Access to this love, the
message implies, can never be shut off, but
always remains open for us to use if we will.

The speaker is direct in his comments, "I
know your works" (Rev. 3:8), so far neither
praising nor blaming, but we are informed
that what we are, what we have done, is no
secret; it shows forth in our life's experience.
Then follows: "Behold, I have set before you
an open door, which no one is able to shut"
(Rev. 3:8). This is a deliberate reiteration of
the never-ending availability of love previously referred to, in order to emphasize its
importance. Whatever our situation, whatever our need, the healing, harmonizing, pros-
pering power of love will always be present

for us to use and to share. From the context it would seem that we have not been loving enough. Of course, we mean well, and have tried to be loving and understanding in our relationships, and the Christ gives us due credit: "I know that you have but little power, and yet you have kept my word and have not denied my name."

Now we have reached the heart of the matter, our scant understanding of the importance and power of love. Love is a much misunderstood word, and indeed its importance has not been fully appreciated. Often confused with the kind of love that derives from the Greek *eros*, the word *love* has been misunderstood and largely discounted as being a desirable quality. It has most often been associated with sexual or possessive love, and is considered to be an unstable and unreliable emotion. However, certainly within the last few decades, the quality of love is increasingly being understood as a strong, durable element, and its power to heal and adjust is now at long last being recognized. At one time, to be considerate, compassionate, and empathetic, that is, loving, was thought of as being weak and effeminate, whereas now it is recognized that these same qualities are, in fact, evidence of strength.

The dilemma of humankind is evidenced by the next statement of the Messenger in which He again refers to those of the synagogue of Satan, first mentioned in His message to the church in Smyrna. This has to do with that part of our thinking which believes it is behaving in a certain way, when in fact our actions belie this. Most of the time people do not fully understand how to express love, nor do they understand the cost to themselves of being unloving. To be completely loving, we need to be unfailingly considerate, kind, forgiving, compassionate, understanding, generous, and completely free from any trace of resentment, recrimination, or desire to get even. If any of these uncharitable concepts occupy our minds, we suffer. It becomes profitable for us to ask ourselves what the challenges are that face us in life at any given moment; for example, a business loss, a financial setback, a problem of human relationships, sickness, accident, or some unexpected glitch in our plans. Perhaps the unsuspected reason for this challenge is to be found in our failure to express enough love.

As we grow in our understanding of Truth, we will learn to love more. We will recall that we, ourselves, are growing, unfolding spiritual beings, and although we have made many mistakes in our lives, we have always acted in accord with the highest good that we knew when all the pressures and circumstances were considered. Through all our continuing errors of commission and omission, the loving First Cause, God, never holds our falling short against us, but exults in our overcomings. So we will now begin to view with new understanding all the people with whom we share our world, and love them in a fresh and undemanding way. We will know that they, too, have always done the best they knew how at the time; we will forgive them and release them to their own Christ presence. We will love them without possession.

To love without possession is not easy. Much of what we call love is really conditional love, whereas true love is always unconditional. It is not dependent on the behavior of others. Too often we find ourselves saying, in effect, "I will love you as long as you do the things that earn my love, but if you do not behave as I expect you to, then I cannot love you." It is this kind of "watery glue" that fails so lamentably to "cement" many couples together in marriage.

We should recall that every thought or feeling we have falls on one side or the other of

the "continental divide" of love or hate, of
life and death. If we approve a thing, in effect, we desire it to continue to exist, or we
love it. On the other hand, anything we do not
care for, consciously or unconsciously, we
wish to be removed from our experience, that
is, to "die," or we "hate" it. The presence in
our consciousness of this "hate" or "wish it
would die" element can color or infect our attitude toward life as a whole, and so every
area of our experience is affected.

A man came to me for counsel because his
business was failing and his health was suffering. In conversation I learned that he had
a very poor relationship not merely with his
competitors, but also with his own business
associates who, he felt, were undermining his
efforts. He was at war with his world. My
counsel to him was to love all the people in his
circle, otherwise his resentment would destroy him. However, in his case, the word
love had to be re-expressed, as it had all the
wrong connotations for him. First, he had to
begin to understand the reasons for his associates' behavior and recognize that they were
being human in trying to get ahead, just as
he was. I advised him to bless them, begin to
appreciate their qualities, and be considerate
of their needs. Then I urged him to show true

love to his competitors by praying for their success in business, with the knowledge that there was enough work for them all, and to rejoice in their success. This last suggestion caused him to choke and splutter, but he finally understood that to enjoy the unlimited blessings which God desired to bestow on him, he had first to recognize the necessity of allowing the love of God to work in and through him. He agreed to spend thirty minutes every day in prayer, enfolding himself and all his associates and competitors in waves of love. Later, he reported that despite the difficulties in actually spending this time daily, he had persisted most days, and stated he felt better and happier, and business was improving immeasurably.

Jesus attached so much importance to love that He gave us a new commandment, "That you love one another" (Jn. 13:34). Psychologists attribute many of the behavior quirks of individuals to the fact that they were unloved, or at least *felt* unloved, as children. But the great need of humankind is not so much to be loved as it is that we should learn to love more.

On one occasion another man sought my counsel because of his inability to hold jobs. He stated he was unable to relate to older men, and that most of his bosses had been older men. After close questioning, he recognized that this was because they reminded him of his father. He said he did not love his father, who had favored his brothers, and over the years his resentment had grown almost to hatred. I counseled him to forgive his father. He regretted it was now too late as his father had passed on. "It is not too late. Let us speak to him in prayer." We became still, and in prayer spoke words of forgiveness to his father. Afterward, the man felt at peace and said that at last he felt he had forgiven his dad. With a new understanding of other people he was soon able to obtain a new position in which he advanced rapidly.

This is love, truly the very essence of God, yet also a practical and dynamic tool available for all humankind. Emmet Fox wrote, "There is no difficulty that enough love will not conquer; no disease that enough love will not heal; no door that enough love will not open" (*Power Through Constructive Thinking*).

In a moment of reflection we realize how wonderfully the Comforter works in having placed this message addressed to our love center immediately following that directed to the church of Sardis, or our realization of the inherent powers that we all have. Having first understood that it is our responsibility and privilege to use our inner powers, we are now reminded of the need to express love, the greatest power of all.

Gold Refined by Fire

Revelation 3:14-22

When addressing the angel of the church in Laodicea, the last of the seven churches, the Christ presence returns to the theme with which Jesus opened His Sermon on the Mount: "Blessed are the poor in spirit, for theirs is the kingdom of heaven" (Mt. 5:3). While this may not be immediately obvious to the casual reader, it becomes clear as we study the underlying meaning of Laodicea. Incidentally, the inclusion of this principle at this stage underlines the necessity of this concept being fully grasped and implemented by the spiritual wayfarer. The importance of this principle is enhanced when we consider the manner in which the Christ introduces Himself: "The words of the Amen, the faithful and true witness, the beginning of God's creation" (Rev. 3:14). Amen, or so be it; this is so now, and always shall be; on this authority the universe was created. The principle is inescapable. It applies inexorably.

The name *Laodicea* means "justice," or "judgment of the people." Its metaphysical meaning is "a phase of the judgment faculty expressing in the personal, which bases its decisions on the intellectual." We derive a better understanding of the character of the Laodicean when we remind ourselves of the city's history. Laodicea was an extremely wealthy and influential industrial center, the financial and banking hub for the region and the home of a prominent medical school and research center. The city was so rich and self-sufficient that in the year A.D. 60, when it was extensively damaged by an earthquake, the citizens rejected the help of the emperor of Rome to rebuild it. When this experience is coupled with the metaphysical meaning of the word, the key idea of *self-sufficiency in the intellectual sense* is revealed. This letter is addressed to us when in consciousness we have come to rely too heavily, or perhaps exclusively, on human wisdom instead of habitually turning to the Christ for guidance. In the spiritual sense we have become arrogant,

or humanly self-sufficient, rather than remaining "poor in spirit," which, as Jesus
said, is the way to the kingdom of heaven.

The message begins with the now familiar
words, "I know your works." What we are
cannot be concealed. The message continues
provocatively, "You are neither cold nor
hot . . . . So, because you are lukewarm, and
neither cold nor hot, I will spew you out of my
mouth." The term "neither cold nor hot" suggests vacillation, a wavering nature, the inability to arrive at decisions. We recall the
metaphysical meaning of Laodicea: judgment
of the people, making decisions based on the
intellectual. This suggests a tendency to ask
the opinions of others, to seek their advice, to
want to act in a way approved by others. The
result of this is to be "spewed out of the
mouth," which is a graphic way of describing
a sense of rejection by life. (We become "sick
of life" and life becomes "sick of us.")

Christ continues: "For you say, I am rich, I
have prospered, and I need nothing; not
knowing that you are wretched, pitiable,
poor, blind, and naked" (Rev. 3:17). In a
material sense we may well be rich and intel-
lectually knowledgeable, and this can lull us
into a sense of self-sufficiency. But our trust
in the outer is misplaced. By relying on the

counsel of the worldly-wise, by judging only by appearances, we may one day find ourselves, in the figurative sense if not literally, "wretched, pitiable, poor, blind, and naked." For truly our dependence should be on God. We should always acknowledge the indwelling Spirit as the one source of wisdom, supply, and healing. We should always seek His guidance.

We are then counseled by the Christ to obtain from Him gold refined by fire. This implies the true riches of the spirit, from which all the dross of self-interest, desire to please others, and fear of making decisions has been burned away. From this same source we receive "white garments" or the purity of purpose and intention. These protect us from the embarrassment of being revealed as hollow and ill-considered in our judgments and actions. Also, ours is "salve for the eyes," or spiritual insight, the ability to judge all people, conditions, and situations "righteously."

Fortunately, at any time, we can repent, change our superficial way of thinking, and turn within to the Christ, who assures us: "Behold, I stand at the door and knock . . ." The counsel of the Christ is always available to all who will become still and seek His guidance in prayer and meditation. At any time that we conquer the tendency to seek counsel in the outer and decide to live our lives under the direction of the indwelling Christ, we will be able to exert new dominion and control (sit on His throne) and truly find the kingdom of heaven on this plane, in the here and now.

This calls for constant vigilance over our thoughts, feelings, words, and actions, which can only be attained by our frequently entering into the consciousness of the Sabbath. Charles Fillmore states, "The true Sabbath is that state of spiritual attainment where man rests from all personal effort and all belief in his own works, and rests in the consciousness that 'the Father abiding in me doeth his works' (Jn. 14:10 A.V.). The Sabbath is kept any time we enter into spiritual consciousness and rest from thoughts of temporal things. We let go of the external observance of days, because every day is a Sabbath on which we retire into Spirit and worship God" (*The Revealing Word*).

The follower of the Way, when facing decisions of any sort, is well advised to turn within and enter the consciousness of the Sabbath when seeking direction. Ideally, it should be customary to take a regular time of prayer and meditation at the start of each day; the wayfarer can then quickly and un-ceremoniously enter a brief moment of inner turning sufficient to allow the inner contact to be made. It is then important to heed the guidance that is given and to act on this un-hesitatingly in the face of any counsel offered by others.

It cannot be stated too often or too emphat-ically that it is the divine intention that hu-mankind should at all times turn to Spirit for direction. "In the beginning God ... " This should be our immediate impulse—turn first to God for direction, and then to man or take other steps as we are prompted. Paul wrote, "For the wisdom of this world is folly with God" (1 Cor. 3:19), and James added: "But the wisdom from above is first pure, then peaceable, gentle, open to reason, full of mercy and good fruits, without uncertainty or insincerity" (Jas. 3:17). Let us freely admit that, humanly, neither we nor others know for certain what is the best course in a situa-tion, for the information we have is limited. But Spirit, Omniscience, does know. It is es-sential for our spiritual growth that we make a habit of obtaining spiritual direction our-selves, and then acting decisively on the di-rection given. Following this counsel is the sure way to finding the kingdom.

The Template

The Churches Reviewed

Before proceeding with our spiritual journey to the New Jerusalem as outlined in The Revelation to John, it will be profitable to review our progress thus far. The Christ presence has lovingly but penetratingly observed our spiritual progress. He has praised our successes and shown us where change is needed if we are to find the kingdom. Perhaps not all the comments that have been made apply to every one of us, but certainly we are wise if we will engage in some introspection to see if and where change is needed. In meditation we should prayerfully contemplate (come together with the template—the pattern) the state of our souls. Let us then review the messages to the angels that overlook the seven areas of our spiritual endeavor.

First, has the sparkle gone out of life? Has our spiritual progress become drudgery? If so, the reason probably lies in our failure to see good in every situation. We must learn to love God, to love all of life more. We must seek the blessing in every happening. A blessing is there, because God is there. Then we will find that every event, both good and so-called evil, nourishes and feeds us and opens the way to lasting joy.

Second, are we consciously or unconsciously seeking material prosperity and success as ends in themselves, instead of seeking first the kingdom? By seeking to attain oneness with God, our one and only source, we will find all our needs richly and abundantly met. Our part is to maintain a positive attitude and see ourselves as free-flowing channels of God's abundant supply into all our world.

Third, have we wandered off the highway of spiritual growth and strayed into bypaths of peripheral teachings? These may well be interesting but will not of themselves assist us along the road to higher consciousness. Our objective should continually be that of attaining the awareness of our oneness with God through our recognition of the I AM.

Fourth, are we exhibiting any tendency to become overzealous in our own religious observance and possibly imposing our concepts on others, or are we becoming intolerant of the religious beliefs of others? We are warned that these tendencies are counterproductive and will cause us great tribulation. We are counseled to stress our own progress and free others to their own indwelling Christ.

Fifth, are we aware of and using our own indwelling spiritual powers? There is within each of us the precious gem of dominion, and if we fail to avail ourselves of this, we condemn ourselves to a life of frustration. The answer is to exercise our spiritual faculties and take charge of our own destiny, and so enjoy the rich and fulfilling life.

Sixth, are we aware of and using the greatest of all those inherent powers—love? As we increasingly come into the realization of ourselves as growing, unfolding spiritual beings, and recognize that our loving God has never condemned us, nor held any of our mistakes or shortcomings against us, so we understand that this is true of all other people, and that we must forgive all people all things, and love them without possession.

Seventh, and finally, are we in the habit of

consulting others for advice and counsel? Remember, the Bible opens with the words, "In the beginning God" (Gen. 1:1). Our first step should always be to go to God. The Way-Shower opened His Sermon on the Mount with the statement: "Blessed are the poor in spirit" (Mt. 5:3). We exhibit this humility of spirit when we recognize that God's wisdom is greater than human knowledge, however rich, profound, and learned this knowledge may be. The way to assume the throne and take control of our lives is to first consult the presence of God indwelling.

Having examined ourselves in the light of the foregoing, we are now ready for the next step, that of recommitment. The reader may have noted that the Christ has touched on seven major areas in which the spiritual seeker is prone to fall short. In so doing He has seemingly been selective. He did not, for example, go through the entire Decalogue. This has been regarded as being God's law, and surely should have been considered. The reader may have discerned that in essence the first four commandments were touched on. The first, "You shall have no other gods before me" (Ex. 20:3), runs through all the messages. The second, "You shall not make for yourself a graven image" (Ex. 20:4), is im-

plied in the message to Smyrna. The third,
"You shall not take the name of . . . your God
in vain" (Ex. 20:7), is emphasized throughout
in the warnings to avoid misuse of the I AM.
And the fourth, "Remember the sabbath"
(Ex. 20:8), is covered in the message to Laodicea, recognizing that the Sabbath is any
time devoted exclusively to Spirit. But the remaining six have seemingly been neglected.

We have perceived a reason for this. The
Decalogue comprises the universal laws of
life that must be observed by all individuals if
they desire to live a full and satisfying life.
These are common to all humankind, regardless of their religious beliefs. The Revelation
to John, on the other hand, is directed to a
very special group of individuals—those who
are committed to following the Jesus Christ
teachings to higher consciousness. The
Christ presence assumes that the follower of
His way will already have overcome the
grosser forms of unsocial behavior that are
the subject of the last six commandments.
Anyway, all these are embraced by His teaching of love, about which He gave us His new
commandment.

As we turn to examine the remainder of
The Revelation to John, it should again be
stated that the events described are the inner

experiences of the souls of deeply committed individuals as they continue on the path of spiritual growth. The book will remain a mystery for most people until they, too, become aware of the inner prompting for reunion with their Source. Earnest spiritual seekers, however, deliberately elect to take the upward path in response to the longing of the soul and the prompting of the Christ. To them The Revelation to John will have a deep and precious meaning. None of the events mentioned are factual, but their effect on the individual is nonetheless real. The agonies and torments later described must indeed be the lot of earnest pilgrims if they are hesitant or halfhearted in their progress. There will be the constant tug of the old way of thinking and believing, and this will hinder our speedy progress unless we consciously "let go and let God." It is said, "Resistance creates friction, and friction creates heat." It is our resistance to change that will be creating any heat or pain that we experience.

In our evolution through successive life experiences, our souls (our conscious and subconscious minds) have accumulated many concepts that probably were important to our continued existence at a particular time. They were appropriate when we lived on a more material and grossly physical level, but we are now seeking to move to a higher dimension of thinking and living. We have been earthbound for too long. If we are to free ourselves from the gravitational pull of the old way of merely existing, and attain the weightlessness of spiritual living, we must jettison the support systems we have long relied on. This will involve our readiness to throw over many of our cherished beliefs, fears, and comfort zones, and step out into a new dimension of faith and trust. Again, this will cause us pain to the degree that we resist change.

This is the purpose of The Revelation to John. This is its value—both its timelessness and its timeliness. The spiritual wayfarer of any age or time is able to go forward fearlessly in the knowledge that the beast, the devil, Satan, and whatever else may lie ahead, are but the illusory products of our own fearful imaginings and have no reality of themselves. The plagues and woes foreshadowed are but the products of our own vacillation and hesitancies, and we have no need to experience them.

The following chapters of The Revelation to John outline in symbolic form the challenges that await us, and culminate in the transcendent consciousness that must be ours as we overcome. Let us, therefore, consciously recommit ourselves to following the Jesus Christ way to higher consciousness and claim citizenship in the kingdom.

Victorious Living

Revelation 4

"After this I looked, and lo, in heaven an open door!" (Rev. 4:1) In the fourth chapter we are given an insight to the glory that awaits us. John is told, "Come up hither, and I will show you what must take place after this" (Rev. 4:1). Freely translated, this means that this is what you will experience after you have obtained the victory over the tendencies and temptations previously outlined in the seven areas of spiritual observance; or, this will be your nature after you have made the adjustments contained in the seven messages.

Verses two through six are worthy of close study, for they contain a vision of transcendent glory. This is the spiritual destiny of humankind when regeneration is complete. An open door to heaven! In a moment of spiritual insight we are allowed a rare glimpse of the glory that awaits us. There we see a throne on which is seated one who appears like jasper and carnelian, and around the throne is a rainbow that looks like an emerald. John was attempting to put into words what probably was a blaze of glorious light. How better can one describe the illumined spirit of regenerated man when consciously reunited with Christ? No longer is there any sense of separation, for man is now completely at one with Source.

From the throne there issue flashes of lightning and peals of thunder, illustrating power over elemental forces. The idea of completion is conveyed by the presence of the seven torches of fire. "Before the throne there is as it were a sea of glass, like crystal" (Rev. 4:6). To be "before the throne" indicates harmony with all that is on the throne or that emanates from the throne; the sea indicates limitless possibilities for growth.

The vision continues: "Round the throne were twenty-four thrones, and seated on the thrones were twenty-four elders, clad in white garments, with golden crowns upon their heads" (Rev. 4:4). It should be noted that twenty-four is twice twelve, and twelve is the number of spiritual completion. This takes us back to the prophecy of Jesus, "Truly, I say to you, in the new world, when the Son of man shall sit on his glorious throne, you who have followed me will also sit on twelve thrones, judging the twelve tribes of Israel" (Mt. 19:28). The Son of man is the I AM in man, and it is the intention that we should put the I AM, the awareness of the Christ presence, on the throne of our lives. To do this we must attain mastery over our twelve mental faculties. These twelve faculties have been identified by Charles Fillmore: faith, strength, judgment, love, power, imagination, understanding, will, order, enthusiasm, renunciation, and life. These twelve powers which are inherent in all humankind will, in the process of regeneration, have been lifted up and refined. Thus, they are increased in effect and power and represented in the vision as twenty-four (double their number) elders (indicating maturity), each seated on a throne (evidence of their power and authority). These are all subject to the overarching authority of the Son of man, the one seated on the central throne. Each of the elders is clad in white garments (indicating their innate purity and immaculate judgment) and wears a golden crown (revealing priceless and lasting wisdom).

The vision included four living creatures that stood around the throne. The first was like a lion, the second was like an ox, the third had the face of a man, and the fourth was like a flying eagle. These four creatures represent the four broad aspects of humankind: the lion stands for the physical nature of humankind; the ox, for our strong emotional urges; that with the face of a man, human intelligence and thinking capacity; and that like a flying eagle, the aspiring and inspirational tendencies. Each of these creatures is described as being full of eyes in front and behind, all around and within, and each has six wings.

As we become familiar with the symbolism used by the inspired writer, we recognize that these are human aspects that have now become spiritualized, and the eyes signify the existence of foresight, hindsight, and insight, or perfect vision and understanding. That the creatures have six wings reveals their ability to soar above the material and mundane, to attain great heights of spirituality.

The chapter concludes on a note of high praise as the living creatures and the twenty-four elders are reported as ceaselessly lauding and adoring the occupant of the throne.

This sublime note is a justifiable description of the regenerated consciousness, the consciousness that has succeeded in spiritualizing the four basic areas of human nature. This is a valid description of the awareness and outlook of individuals who have conquered their physical nature and have overcome the temptation to strike back; of those who are in control of their emotions, having attained mastery over the storms of anger, resentment, jealousy, and fear; of those who are no longer coldly calculating and unfeeling in their judgments and do not base decisions on material considerations; and of those who have true spiritual aspirations. This vision beautifully describes in symbolic form the mind of those who, truly adoring God, are able to soar above personal and material considerations, gifted with divine insight into the needs and points of view of others. Such people see all the world with nonpossessive and undemanding love and compassion. They are able to rise above all the minor and major vexations that might once have thrown them. They are overcomers.

Overcomers, in their heart of hearts, never cease to sing, "Holy, holy, holy, is the Lord God Almighty" (Rev. 4:8). This is the welling up of praise and thanksgiving from the depths of being. This is the spontaneous commentary of those who are deeply enjoying a wholly fulfilling life experience. It is a song that is born of a sense of wonder and gratitude for the unfailing goodness and richness of God and life, and it cannot be silenced. This is the consciousness we seek. In the words of Shakespeare's Hamlet: " 'Tis a consummation devoutly to be wished." In the following section we are told what we must do next to attain this very desirable state of mind.

The Lamb Is Worthy

Revelation 5

The vision continues into the fifth chapter. "And I saw in the right hand of him who was seated on the throne a scroll written within and on the back, sealed with seven seals; and I saw a strong angel proclaiming with a loud voice, 'Who is worthy to open the scroll and break its seals?' . . . and I wept much that no one was found worthy to open the scroll or to look into it" (Rev. 5:1-4). The Christ is seated on the throne, and in His right hand, the hand of power, is every individual's book of life.

The Christ knows us as does nobody else. The Christ knows us in a way that even we do not know ourselves. Here in the scroll is written the truth about ourselves as we are now, the true state of our souls; our strengths, our weaknesses, our innermost fears, unsuspected paranoias, subconscious beliefs, neuroses, quirks, hang-ups, foibles, all our complexes. Here in symbol form are recorded all the underlying causes, usually unconscious, that result in our being intolerant, insecure, fearful, apprehensive, bigoted, prejudiced, and unhappy. Here are the deeply buried reasons for our greed, anger, flashes of irritation, jealousy, and cruelty. If we could discover these, if they could be revealed to us, our spiritual journey would be much easier. But, alas, the scroll is secured by seven seals. Small wonder that we weep when we realize how seemingly inaccessible are the reasons for our failure to overcome.

We long to move out into the new dimension of joyous living that we know instinctively can be ours. We yearn to make our faith active and to revel in the peace of mind, the radiant health and freedom from want that we know to be God's will and desire for us, but like Paul, we find ourselves doing the things we should not do, and leaving undone those things we should do. Indeed, the spirit is willing, but the flesh is weak. Sudden flashes of unreasoning anger and thoughtless, unkind responses perplex us; they grieve us. Why do we behave so? What makes us eat or drink excessively, or behave in ways that are unacceptable to ourselves? What makes us addicts? We do not know the unconscious drives that from time to time result in unsocial and damaging surface responses. The reasons are hidden from us, secured by seven seals. Something within us weeps at our frustration.

But there is hope! There is a way. "Then one of the elders said to me, 'Weep not; lo, the Lion of the tribe of Judah, the Root of David, has conquered, so that he can open the scroll and its seven seals' " (Rev. 5:5). Then, "I saw a Lamb standing, as though it had been slain . . . and he went and took the scroll" (Rev. 5:6-7). There follows a period in which the elders, the living creatures and myriads of angels join in a mighty anthem, "Worthy is the Lamb who was slain, to receive power and wealth and wisdom and might and honor and glory and blessing!" (Rev. 5:12) In this they are joined by every creature in the universe.

Yes, there is hope, and the solution lies in our discovering the qualities within ourselves that are necessary to the opening of the scroll. In prayer we find that The Revelation to John is unusually explicit on this point. There are five main qualities described. First, the Lion suggests courage and fearlessness. Second, it is no ordinary lion, but the Lion of Judah, and Judah means to have reverence for spiritual things. Third, the Root of David is the love quality from whose house sprang Jesus. Fourth, the Lamb suggests meekness, willingness to follow. Finally, the reference to the Lamb's having been slain suggests the necessity of sacrifice.

This is what it takes to gain true insight into one's self: a combination of courage to examine one's own thought processes fearlessly, true love and reverence for things of the spirit, love of the Jesus Christ teachings coupled with a meekness to admit one's own mistakes, harmless and inoffensive judgments of others, and willingness to sacrifice ego in order to gain spiritual insight and growth.

Here is one of the great promises of the Bible. If we will bring together a deep yearning for spirituality, fearlessness in facing our own shortcomings, the meekness to admit them, the courage to deal with them, and love for all, then we will inherit the kingdom and rule over our own private world.

In all this, let us not overlook the poignant reference to the "Lamb standing as though it had been slain," slain presumably on the altar of sacrifice. This is a telling analogy. We can open the scroll if we bring together in prayer and silence the qualities mentioned and ask the Christ to tell us where we have failed. Then we must wait long enough to allow the absolutely impartial and penetrating answers to flood in, telling us where we have been unloving, thoughtless, cruel, egotistical, resentful, gossipy, revengeful, dishonest, competitive, ambitious, greedy, and so on. We must ask the Christ, and if we are sincere, He will tell us. Let us write down what He tells us. Then ask Him what we should do about each item. We should write that down too. Perhaps He wants us to make an apology, to be honest with someone, to make some restitution. We should obey the suggestions we have received. If we do this, we will know how it feels to be "as though slain." For as Jesus said: "The gate is narrow and the way is hard, that leads to life, and those who find it are few" (Mt. 7:14).

A woman called my office, demanding to see me. She was in great pain. Her prescription pain relievers had become ineffective. She was crying and moaning and talking of taking her own life, so I said, "Come right over." She arrived dishevelled and not properly dressed, but she appeared neither to know nor care. She was constantly wracked with great waves of pain that convulsed her. She was almost incoherent—she had taken many of her painkillers and these had caused her to be confused, but had left the pain untouched. She talked disjointedly about the physical causes—some earlier surgery, then renewed surgery to deal with adhesions, now this renewed agony when her physician could find no physical cause. Would I please treat for the removal of the pain?

I talked briefly about the futility of suicide, then about the necessity of loving and forgiving other people. Then I prayed with her, and as we prayed we recognized the forgiving love and healing power of God. She continued to moan and writhe as successive spasms swept over her. I led her in a drill of relaxation, and prayed for love and harmony. I could not reach her. I prayed aloud. I prayed in the silence. I endeavored to behold her as a perfect child of God in a perfect universe. I affirmed her complete healing. I declared she was at peace, at ease, all to no avail. I continued to pray in the silence. "God, show us. What is the key to her pain? What must she do? What can I do? Heal her, God; let Your perfect healing, loving work be done in and through her. Merciful God, why should she suffer this pain?" I rested in the silence, baffled, frustrated, not knowing what more to do. Then I got a single idea; perhaps it was a word in reply. Injury. Injury? Yes, injury is the cause. Injury causes pain. Suddenly light dawned. Of course, injury causes pain!

I asked her, "Have you injured other people? Have you caused other people to have pain?"

Still crying and rocking in her chair, she whispered, "Yes, many people. I have caused much pain to others."

"In the past, or recently?"

"Both, I've always hurt people. But I had to, to survive. I was not wanted. People hurt me—so I hurt them back."

So I said to her. "Think back to the last person you hurt, and in the silence, say to him or her, 'I'm sorry I caused you pain. Please forgive me. I forgive you. I'm sorry I caused you pain.' " Without speaking aloud, she nodded assent, and I saw her lips moving as she appeared to be repeating the statement over and over.

After a little time, I said, "Now think back to the next previous person you hurt and say in the silence, 'I'm sorry I hurt you. I didn't know any better. Please forgive me.' " Again, she appeared to do as suggested. Then we went back over her life in five-year periods, and included specifically her father and mother, her ex-husband and siblings, forgiving and asking forgiveness. It took time, but throughout she was growing progressively quieter. Finally, she was still.

After an interval she looked up and said, "Mr. Neal, I think my pain has gone. I just feel terribly tired. Thank you."

I replied, "I am so grateful and happy for you. Now, do you think there is anything you should do?"

"Do?" she asked. "I don't think I understand."

"Well, it is nice that your pain has gone, but it might return. Have you really forgiven those people whom you thought hurt you? Do they know you have forgiven them? And do you think you should ask their forgiveness?"

There was a long pause. At length she said, "Yes, perhaps there is something I should do. Some of them are dead now and it's too late, but I should speak to certain people and write to others. It will be difficult to face them, but I feel I should do it."

My counselee stood before the ever open door of love and forgiveness. It was now up to her to decide whether or not to have the courage to sacrifice her ego and follow the example of the Lamb that had been slain. She should now know that injury causes pain, that forgiveness begets forgiveness, that like produces like. It is an immutable law. Now she had to face the cost and become as a lamb that has been slain. If she followed through on her guidance to forgive and ask forgiveness she would find her freedom. She would experience for herself the fruits of the promise: "Worthy is the Lamb who was slain to receive power and wealth and wisdom and might and honor and glory and blessing!" What more can one ask?

Joy or Misery?

Revelation 6:1-8

Chapter six records the Lamb starting to open the seals. It is suggested that the reader read the first seven verses of this chapter. In summary, the text states that as the Lamb opened each of the first four seals, a different one of the four living creatures spoke, and there emerged, in turn, four horses with riders. The first was a white horse, the second a red horse, the third a black horse, and the fourth a pale horse. The four horses are extensions of the properties of the living creatures that uttered the command, "Come!" But this time we meet them in a different order.

In chapter four, the living creature first mentioned was like a lion representing our physical nature, the second like an ox representing our emotions, the third with a face like a man representing the human intellect, and the fourth like an eagle representing our aspiration to spiritual heights. This is the order in which humankind first becomes aware of itself—first as a body that needs food and shelter; second as an emotional being that loves, hates, and fears; third as an intellect that is capable of thinking and reasoning; and last when we become aware of our spiritual needs.

But now, the order has changed. The Lamb, representing the enlightened consciousness, demonstrates that the way to triumphant living is for the individual to first become aware of himself or herself as a spiritual entity. So the first rider to emerge is appropriately astride a white horse, signifying purity. He has a bow and a crown indicating his ability to be victorious and to rule. The one enemy to inflict a resounding defeat on the Roman legions was the Parthians, mounted bowmen. So the clear message here is: Put first in your life the understanding of your spiritual nature and you will be victorious. Primarily, you are a spiritual being!

The second horse to emerge was bright red, indicating the vital part played by the control of our emotions. (We "see red" when angry.)

"Its rider was permitted to take peace from the earth, so that men should slay one another" (Rev. 6:4). Note carefully that this is not a dire prediction that war and death by the sword must necessarily come, but is a revelation of the potential danger inherent in uncontrolled emotions. The "earth" in this context is man's personal world, his life experience. Uncontrolled emotions can lead to words and actions that are afterward regretted, and peace of mind is lost.

John Smith, a member of my congregation in a northeastern city, was employed by one of the big automakers. He was a big, powerful man who was frequently getting into arguments, and sometimes fistfights, with other employees. He came to see me at his wife's urging, as she was afraid that his short fuse would get him into real trouble and possibly cost him his job. John was not a bit repentant or contrite, for most of the time he firmly believed he was right.

He said, "You know, Mr. Neal, I'm a proud man, and I'm not going to let any no-good so-and-so push me around, foreman or no foreman." He reminded me, "It says in the Psalms, 'I'll make your enemies your footstool,' and that's what I'm going to do. As for getting fired, I'm a strong union man, and the union won't let them fire me." I counseled moderation and prayed with him, but knew I had not reached him.

Some months later he returned, this time of his own volition. He was scared. He had had an argument with a union official, and losing his temper, had knocked him down. This time the union was not about to intercede on his behalf. Would I please pray with him? I did, but first I lectured him and referred him to the psalm he had mentioned. I read aloud to him the first verse, "The Lord says to my lord: 'Sit at my right hand, till I make your enemies your footstool' " (Ps. 110:1). I explained to him the meaning. "God is saying to the ruling element in you, sit at my right hand, that is, obey my commandments, until you have control of your enemies. Your enemies are not other people—fellow workers, foremen, or union officials. Your enemies are your own violent thoughts and emotions. Get control of yourself, admit the possibility that you could be wrong, and in any event don't let anger get the better of you or it will be your undoing. He who lives by the sword shall die by the sword, but be peaceful, and you will be at peace. The choice is yours." He saw the point. We prayed together for patience, love, and self-control. So much was at stake that he decided to apologize to the other man, and the affair blew over and he kept his job. From that time on, he worked at controlling his temper.

We are our own worst enemy—our only enemy, in fact. Once we have learned to bring our emotions under control and no longer allow anger, resentment, fear, jealousy, hatred, and the like to master us, we will discover the secret of peace and harmony in our personal world.

The rider of the black horse represents the intellect, that in us which reasons and bargains, as indicated in verses five and six. Our intellect is a wonderful tool. There is nothing wrong with being well-informed. However, it is essential that the intellect always be subject to Spirit. This is best ensured by regularly taking time for prayer and meditation. To allow material aspects to dominate one's life will surely lead to an unbalanced life experience in which true values are missed and frustration and emptiness become our lot.

With the opening of the fourth seal, the pale horse emerges, "and its rider's name was Death, and Hades followed him; and they were given power over a fourth of the earth, to kill..." (Rev. 6:8). It is an arresting realization to be faced with the fact that in truth the physical nature of humankind is fourth in line of importance and so is the last to emerge! This time the physical nature is represented as Death, or being terminated. Again, it should be emphasized that all consideration of the physical nature and its well-being should be subject to the direction of Spirit.

Significantly, Death rides the pale horse symbolizing fear. When a person is fearful the color drains from the face, leaving him ashen, pale. There is an almost universal fear of death. Humankind harbors many fears, but probably the greatest of these is that of death. This is due to ignorance of the essential continuity of life. In Truth, there is no death. There are changes of condition, the transition from one bodily form to another form, but the human spirit cannot be extinguished. The I AM is indestructible and is timeless, ageless, and literally deathless.

A right concept of both life and its apparent opposite, death, is essential to truly enjoy this earthly experience. Traditionally death is feared because it appears to be the end of everything for that individual. However, life is continuous and consciousness persists beyond the grave. We are all growing, evolving spiritual beings. We have possibly been in and out of the physical body many times over in countless ages, and doubtless will continue to do so until we have evolved beyond the necessity for physical experience. As we come to realize that so-called death is as natural and as much a part of life as is birth, then we will accept this inevitable change for the boon it truly is.

Death occurs, early or late, when the soul knows that it has completed its present self-imposed mission on this plane. The entity goes forward, free from all the limitations of the gross physical body, and steps out into the freedom of the next plane, light and unrestricted. This knowledge, deeply inculcated into the consciousness, takes all the fear out of passing. Paul was able to write triumphantly, "O death, where is thy victory? O death, where is thy sting?" (1 Cor. 15:55) However, very few truly believe this. For most people it is a step into the unknown. Add to this the mischievous teaching of a single life experience of seventy years (give or take a few) during which time the individual makes decisions that may result in his possibly being consigned to an eternity of torment, and there is small cause to wonder at the widespread fear of death.

The pain experienced by those left behind

at the separation from a loved one is tremendously lessened when this great universal spiritual Truth has become part of the philosophy of the bereaved. It should be of great comfort to know that the loved one has passed beyond physical pain.

We are told "Hades followed him; and they were given power over a fourth of the earth" (Rev. 6:8). Hades is not something to be feared. In biblical times it was a place where garbage was disposed of. This symbolizes the opportunity to purify our minds and transmute the prevailing fear of death that spoils the last quarter of many people's lives (a fourth part of the earth) into the realization that we are eternal, ever-evolving, spiritual beings. As part of this cleansing process, the memory is purged of all recollection of its mistakes and misdeeds. Thus, our mental garbage is effectively destroyed, leaving us free to take the next joyous steps in God's great and ever-expanding universe of spiritual growth.

"I Will Repay"

Revelation 6:9-11

The Lamb then opens the fifth seal, and John states, "I saw under the altar the souls of those who had been slain for the word of God and for the witness they had borne; they cried out with a loud voice, 'O Sovereign Lord, holy and true, how long before thou wilt judge and avenge our blood on those who dwell upon the earth?' " (Rev. 6:9-10) Let us recall that the opening of the seals symbolizes the uncovering of the contents of our subconscious minds. The unconscious elements in our makeup hold us back in our spiritual growth. The breaking of the fifth seal marks an important revelation of our little-known inner self.

These "souls that had been slain" are the

recollections, both consciously and sub-consciously held, of the injuries we have received in the past. They may cover a wide variety of incidents in our lives, including injustices, bad treatment, or letdowns we have received at the hands of others. The perpetrators may include parents, children, spouses, ex-spouses, lovers, old bosses, employees, fellow workers, or possibly just "the system." Years after the events themselves, the happenings still have the power to cause deep resentment and anger; the festering resentment still causes smarting and pain. The memory of these events rankles, and something within us calls out for justice.

"O Sovereign Lord, holy and true, how long before thou wilt judge and avenge our blood?" But the incidents are in the past. They are under the altar, symbolizing that they are dead and should be buried. By our recollection and our resentment of them, we have created ghosts to haunt us. We have given them the power to spoil our lives. They are under the altar, and the altar implies sacrifice. We should sacrifice them. Give them up, forgive, forget, and be free!

The great love and wisdom of the Comforter are expressed when we read, "Then they were each given a white robe and told to rest a little longer, until the number of their fellow servants and their brethren should be complete, who were to be killed as they themselves had been" (Rev. 6:11). What a beautiful way to express the operation of divine justice at work in every individual's life. In symbolic language we are told, "Here is a white robe, cleanse and purify your mind. Rest and be comforted in the complete assurance that all is well, for just as you were treated, so they will be treated. Justice will work unfailingly, inexorably, and inevitably." Paul put it this way: "Beloved, never avenge yourselves, but leave it to the wrath of God; for it is written, 'Vengeance is mine, I will repay, says the Lord' " (Rom. 12:19).

This is spiritual law at work. It is unfailing. There is never any reason for any one of us to seek to avenge ourselves, or even to hope for some misfortune to happen to another by way of recompense. Just dismiss the incident, knowing with unshakable faith that divine justice is always at work. It cannot fail.

There is a further consideration. The law of divine justice was working at the time you were allegedly misused. The experience was something that you merited, earned, or invited by your consciousness. The occurrence was unavoidable, as you had made it necessary as a learning experience that you needed. There is no injustice; consciousness always rules!

As for the individuals concerned, they were but the instruments or tools of life that happened to be on hand at that time to mete out the necessary lesson which you had demanded of life. It is vital that every disappointment or setback in life is seen in this way, for so long as any resentment is held, whether it be against another person or against life itself, it is clear that the lesson has not been learned and the needed spiritual growth has not been attained. From this, the unpalatable truth emerges that if we do not forgive and forget, we may well be inviting a repetition of the lesson!

There is still another facet to this gem. The injury received provides an incomparable opportunity for further spiritual growth. Jesus taught, "Do not resist . . . evil. . . . Love your enemies. . . . You . . . must be perfect, as your heavenly Father is perfect" (Mt. 5:39-48). We should be ever mindful of the law of cause and effect, and the injury now provides an unparalleled opportunity to produce more good in one's life by praying for the perpetrator and returning some good for seeming evil.

Early in my ministry I knew a couple. The husband, Wilbur, was an attorney with a very traditional church background. He came to Unity to be with his wife who was a seasoned Truth student. She was happy and outgoing, while he was a dour, morose, somewhat moody man. He became intrigued with our teaching of spiritual law, but had many reservations. As time went on he began to see some sense in our teaching of the law of cause and effect, whereas before he had thought things "just happened." I got to know him better while visiting him in the hospital and at his home after he suffered a heart attack.

On one occasion he began to tell me of the many difficulties he had had to meet in his life. As I listened, I began to get somewhat alarmed at the degree of feeling he put into his story as he related certain incidents, and the part some individuals had played in those events. I did not want him to have another heart attack, and certainly not in my presence, so I interrupted him to say in effect that those events were in the past, dead and gone, and he would be well advised to treat them as such, forgetting them and forgiving the people involved. He responded with increasing heat, and vehemently pointed out the injustices he had suffered.

I was in a dilemma. I did not want to argue with him, because of the possible effect on his health, nor did I want to leave him filled with self-pity and rankling with resentment, for these were clearly part of his troubles. So I hastily agreed that he had been badly treated, and he calmed down somewhat.

Before leaving, I said something like, "Wilbur, in the past you have talked about the operation of the law of cause and effect, but it has been somewhat abstract. Now in the next few days while you have time on your hands, why don't you ask yourself this question: 'Knowing the kinds of effects that I want in my life, what sort of mental causes should I dwell on to get those effects?' "

Soon afterward, Wilbur went back to work and as the months went by, I noticed a change in his demeanor. He lost his moodiness, and he became much more open and friendly. One day I met him downtown, so we had lunch together.

In the course of this he said, "I've never forgotten the suggestion you once made to me that I should ask myself what sort of mental causes I should dwell on in order to achieve the kind of effects in my life that I wanted. I decided that I wanted happy, healthy, joyous effects, so I resolved to begin thinking about happy, healthy, prosperous, and joyous things. I used to spend a lot of time thinking about the past and all the raw deals I had experienced. Well, I finally realized there was no percentage in that line, so I just quit doing it. After all, the past is water over the dam, so I let it go. Now I feel better. You'd never believe the good things that continue to happen to Mary and me. It sure pays to forget the past and think happy thoughts!''

Wilbur's experience is a remarkable illustration of the good things that can happen to any individual who will decide to work with spiritual law. He came to the recognition that dwelling on the misfortunes and unhappy events of the past is not the way to happiness. They are in the past, and should be allowed to remain there. By filling his mind with the thoughts of things that he wanted to enjoy, he was able to produce a satisfying and meaningful life-style.

Surviving Life's Earthquakes

Revelation 6:12-17, and 7

The opening of the sixth seal appeared to trigger a series of major disasters as is recorded in the twelfth and succeeding verses of the sixth chapter. There was a great earthquake and a series of other natural catastrophes in which the whole earth was threatened. All humankind, from the greatest to the lowest, was affected. Kings and slaves alike hid in caves to protect themselves from "the wrath of the Lamb" (Rev. 6:16). This highly imaginative narrative is a graphic description of the way in which humankind is inclined to regard the dire events that from time to time seem to affect us all. It is a highly colored but nonetheless apt depiction of the mental agonies people endure when faced by some of the challenges of life. It is in no way to be regarded as a prediction of events that will occur. The action is all in the minds of those who have incurred the wrath of the Lamb.

To incur the "wrath of the Lamb" implies that we have contravened the Lamb's approved way of life. We recall that the Lamb is a composite of a number of qualities. The Lamb combined the courage of the Lion of Judah, that is, the courage to stand for spiritual principles, with the love and compassion of the house that gave rise to Jesus, and the meekness to sacrifice all for principle. When we fail to live by these exacting standards, seeming catastrophes occur. We have tried to break spiritual law, but the effect is that the law breaks us. No one is immune from this law. When the Lamb's standards are contravened, all people—kings, great men and generals, slaves and free men alike—are subject to the law and react in similar fashion: they try to escape the wrath.

The image of the earthquake is an excellent one. Who in life has not suffered some earth-shaking experience, when the ground on which we stood seemed to tremble, and the house of life that we had so painstakingly built came crashing to the ground? The death of a loved one, a grievous financial loss, a disabling accident, a serious illness, the loss of employment, a brush with the law, a beloved child running away from home—the list of possibilities is endless. Any of these and other misfortunes can leave us shaken, bewildered, uncertain. The sun of life is blotted out. God has seemingly forsaken us. What can we now believe in? Where can we safely stand? Such are the reactions of all who are without spiritual resources.

On reflection, however, we realize that God did not forsake us in our time of challenge. We emerged stronger and more resolute for having endured the challenge. Perhaps we needed to be shaken out of the complacency of the so-called safe and secure, the familiar. Great cities, once overcrowded and badly planned, have been utterly destroyed by earthquake, fire, or bombing, then have been rebuilt, vastly improved. So with the individual, seeming disaster gives us the opportunity to remake and rebuild in a way that is an improvement over the old. The outcome depends upon our attitude.

The ultimate effect of any event in life depends upon the way in which we receive it. The vital question is always: How do I react to what has happened? If we stand foursquare in faith in the ultimate goodness of

God, we will be protected. For the vision continues into chapter seven, where it is revealed that four angels stand, preventing the seeming disaster from utterly destroying our world.

As the new day dawns, 144,000 souls have received the protective seal of God upon their foreheads. This is a parable of quality rather than quantity, for we are told a few verses later, "And behold, a great multitude which no man could number . . . from all tribes and peoples and tongues, standing before the throne and before the Lamb, clothed in white robes" (Rev. 7:9). Who are they? "These are they who have come out of the great tribulation; they have washed their robes and made them white in the blood of the Lamb" (Rev. 7:14).

The number 144,000 is made up of twelve times twelve (the number of our faculties of mind), spiritualized and multiplied to infinity. As it is used here it does not signify a limited specific number. It is symbolic of all those who have changed their way of thinking and living and who are now devoting their lives to expressing the ideas of the Lamb. These would include such concepts as truth, faith, love, mercy, compassion, beauty, joy, forgiveness, and enthusiasm for living the teachings of Jesus Christ. Or, expressed more simply, of taking every event in stride, knowing that there is a good outcome, for God— Good—is in every situation.

It is rewarding to look back over verses nine through twelve. Here this great multitude stands before the throne and before the Lamb and worships God, saying, "Amen! Blessing and glory and wisdom and thanksgiving and honor and power and might be to our God for ever and ever! Amen" (Rev. 7:12). Again, this is an apt description of the spontaneous hymn of praise that wells up from deep within the consciousness of the individual who has triumphantly come through the tribulation. This is the song of the heart which knows that the true road to joy and satisfaction lies in dwelling in the constant companionship of the Lamb. As Paul rightly stated, "Christ in you, the hope of glory" (Col. 1:27).

The concluding verses of the chapter (15-17) comprise an inspiring and heartwarming statement of assurance: the promise of the constant protection of God for all who are "before his throne"; that is, all who seek to live the truth way. "They shall hunger no more, neither thirst any more; the sun shall not strike them, nor any scorching heat. . . .

He will guide them to springs of living water; and God will wipe away every tear from their eyes" (Rev. 7:16-17). This is in no sense meant to imply that the seeker of the Way will be immune from the challenges of life, for these are a necessary part of our unfoldment. It means that with our increased understanding we will no longer feel in any way deprived nor allow ourselves to be "burned up," nor will anything cause us to weep, but we will be able to face all that life presents with equanimity and confidence.

The Silence

Revelation 8:1-5

In chapter eight, the long-awaited moment comes and the last seal is opened. "When the Lamb opened the seventh seal, there was silence in heaven for about half an hour" (Rev. 8:1). Truly, the Bible is a remarkably consistent book. It opens in Genesis with the story of creation, when we are told that on the seventh day, God rested. The seventh step in the creative act is to be silent and rest, to allow the previous actions of mind to come into manifestation. Now, when the seventh seal is opened, we are counseled to be silent.

In the silence we may review what has been revealed to us by the opening of the seven seals. First, we became aware that "I am not my body, but essentially I am spirit." Contrary to our old way of looking at things, when our tendency was to place primary emphasis on our physical nature, we now understand that we should in all things put spiritual growth and development first. In all things we should "seek first the kingdom," and only then will all other needful conditions be met in a way that is truly for our highest good.

Second, we became aware of the necessity of controlling our emotions in all circumstances. When we allow our feelings and unregenerate emotions to run away with us, we are courting inevitable disaster. Anger and violence are the sure invitation for violence in return.

Third, we were made aware that the gifts of mind should always be subject to the direction of the spirit and that we should not live in the material and intellectual consciousness. We should be intuitive rather than intellectual in our approach to life. This realization also demands a loving, generous, and forgiving outlook, one that is unfailingly compassionate and empathetic toward others.

Fourth, it was revealed to us that death of the physical body is not to be feared as the end of life, for consciousness is eternal and continues beyond the grave.

Fifth, we came to understand the danger of holding on to past hurts and grievances, the truth that divine order is always at work, and that the unfailing law of recompense must and will adjust all matters. Further, we learned that injuries present us with an opportunity for additional spiritual growth. We recognize the futility of blaming others, for now we know that the cause of our seeming mistreatment lies within some thought or action of our own in the past.

Sixth, we became aware that in every seeming disaster there is a blessing. Misfortune reveals to us that somewhere we have contravened the way of life prescribed by the Lamb. These same misfortunes unfailingly present us with opportunities to experience great spiritual growth as we seek to discern the hand of God in every occurrence.

Finally, and most important, we have learned that it is necessary to take time in the silence to rest and realize the truth of our oneness with our Source and Creator. Only in the silence can we become aware of our primarily spiritual identity and discover the true nature of the I AM. Thus, we will find a new sense of purpose and the ability to overcome whatever may lie before us.

From the foregoing we have come to understand that life is essentially a learning experience, and that our so-called problems are evidence that in some way we have departed from the nature of the Lamb. These same problems are self-invited lessons to assist us in our development, and they highlight the areas in which we need to change. We have also learned that "earthquakes" provide us with the chance to remake our lives. In the light of this greater understanding of ourselves, and of the nature of life, we are now ready to face the tribulations that the divine author pictures as being the lot of the average unregenerate members of the human race.

The Reason for Suffering

Revelation 8:6-13, 9:1-21

Following John's experience of the thirty-minute silence that followed the opening of the seventh seal, there appeared seven angels, and each was given a trumpet. An angel is a messenger from God, and the possession of the trumpets suggests they were entrusted with messages of more than ordinary importance. However, before they could act, an additional angel equipped with a golden censer (incense burner) and much incense appeared, and a great volume of prayers ascended. Finally, the angel filled the censer with fire and flung it to the earth. This suggests that the events that were to follow could be assuaged through the prayers of the heavenly host and by those on earth as they were cleansed (by fire) in consciousness.

Oddly enough, as each angelic trumpet sounded, instead of receiving blessings, the earth was afflicted with new disasters. At the sounding of the first trumpet, hail and fire mixed with blood fell upon the earth and a third of all vegetation was destroyed. The sounding of the second signaled the explosion of a volcano, and a third of the fish were killed, and one-third of all ships destroyed. At the sound of the third, a star called Wormwood fell upon the earth and poisoned much of the water. The fourth angel blew his trumpet, and the sun and moon and stars were damaged and lost one-third of their light, and the earth was in partial darkness. So far these four catastrophes were events that affected nature, or the externals of life, and only indirectly impinged on humankind.

At this point John observed an eagle flying overhead, crying, "Woe, woe, woe to those who dwell on the earth, at the blasts of the other trumpets which the three angels are about to blow!" (Rev. 8:13) The fifth trumpet then sounded and another star fell and opened the shaft to a bottomless pit from which emerged a hoard of locusts like scorpions, which stung and for five months tortured "those of mankind who have not the seal of

God upon their foreheads" (Rev. 9:4). This is followed by a dozen verses graphically describing the tortures that humankind endured. This, we are told, constituted the first woe, and two woes were still to come! The sixth angel sounded his trumpet, and there appeared a great army of cavalry who slew a third of the inhabitants. This is only part of the second woe, which is to continue for two more chapters!

No reason is given for humankind and the earth being so afflicted. However, it is significant that on at least one of these visitations, those who had the "seal of God upon their foreheads" were spared. From this it must be assumed that those who suffered were those who had not triumphantly endured the tribulation; in other words, they were those who were not spiritually awakened. This is our lot while we are still in the physical and material consciousness. "In the world [worldy consciousness] you have tribulation" (Jn. 16:33). A further fact that emerges is that in every case only a part (one-third) of the earth or humankind suffered. This indicates that our *entire* being is never at risk.

Additionally, we are told that the star that fell from heaven to earth was given the key to the shaft of the bottomless pit from which issued the locusts that stung like scorpions. The discovery that the source of so much torture and pain is the "bottomless pit" is highly significant. The pit is "bottomless," it is a hole that has no foundation, no basis; there is no substance to it. It has no reality. Hence, the creatures that emerge also are without basis or reality. They are the figments of humankind's own fears and evil imaginings. Once we become aware of the nonreality of the causes of suffering, we are able to free ourselves from their power.

It is not necessary for us to remain long in the dark as to why humankind should so suffer. The reason lies in our ignorance of the nature of the universe and the way in which we have persistently misused our minds. This is an orderly universe; it is a mental and spiritual cosmos. It was brought into being by the action of Mind. "In the beginning . . . the Spirit of God was moving over the face of the waters. And God said 'Let there be' " (Gen. 1:1-3). In other words, the Creative Intelligence "thought," and when it had come to a conclusion, it uttered the creative word and the manifest universe came into being. As part of the creative act, God said, "Let us make man in our image, after our likeness; and let them have dominion" (Gen. 1:26).

This same principle has been in operation since the beginning of time, and still operates. It is immutable. It is inexorable. It is unvarying and completely reliable. What we think on will one day come into our experience, modified by every other thought we hold. The result may not be precisely as outlined, but will conform to the color or nature of the parent thought. The underlying law might be expressed as: What we think on grows.

Whether we read the history of nations, or inquire into the behavior patterns of modern man and woman, we find there has been little change in the mentality of humankind. The Bible itself illustrates this. The tone was set early on, when Cain murdered his brother in a fit of jealous rage. Thereafter, the pages are filled with stories of murder, theft, rape, war, slaughter, dishonesty, chicanery, selfishness, double-dealing, adultery, fornication, incest, cruelty, intolerance, prejudice, victimization, exploitation—the list is endless. These characteristics were not peculiar to the Hebrew people. They were common to all the peoples of that day—the Romans, Greeks, Philistines, Egyptians, Amorites, Hittites, and Babylonians, and in fact, the entire human race. And these same "inhuman" but so "human" tendencies that have marked the human race throughout history are also common to modern humanity.

However, before we get too carried away by our enthusiasm to account for these woes, we should remind ourselves that this is a metaphysical interpretation. The woes as described in The Revelation to John are not factual, but are the mental experience of some individuals. Yet the argument still applies. Theologians and philosophers have asked the rhetorical question: "Why should the innocent suffer?" People draw to themselves conditions that are in accord with the tone of their thinking. The woes described are the mental sufferings of those individuals who have allowed their minds to dwell on negative and unhelpful matters. In some cases, the effects are indeed physical and become outpictured as sickness, financial losses, or inharmony in relationships. But the anguish described in The Revelation to John is that which is felt mentally, and which can be overcome by a right mental and spiritual attitude, that is, by adopting the nature of the Lamb.

By now we have realized how important the message is that the angels are trumpeting. It is: "Watch your thinking! Watch your words!" These are the days of which Jesus spoke when He said, "On the day of judgment men will render account for every careless word they utter; for by your words you will be justified, and by your words you will be condemned" (Mt. 12:36-37). Every day is judgment day. Today we are reaping the results of our previous thoughts, words, and actions. By liking or disliking these results, we judge them. We are held responsible for the content of our minds. We may not have initiated thoughts of evil, loss, or violence, but to the degree that we are open to the thinking of the race mind and allow these to become seed thoughts, we make them our own. We need to be selective in our choice of entertainment, for example. To feed our minds a constant diet of television programs or plays exalting suspense, horror, fear, violence, and pain can only result in our inviting like conditions into our own experience.

However, we are able to glean some solace from the two important metaphysical truths that emerge: first, all of the disasters are temporary, and second, none affects all of our being. We are threefold beings of spirit, mind, and body. Our spirit, the I AM, can never suffer. It is our minds and bodies that are vulnerable, and this suffering is transitory. The whole spiritual person cannot be placed at risk. The moment we turn in consciousness and embrace the nature of the Lamb the suffering ceases, although to outer appearances the woe may still be in effect. For this we have the testimony of Jesus as illustrated in the parable of the Prodigal Son: "But while he was yet at a distance, his father saw him and had compassion, and ran and embraced him and kissed him" (Lk. 15:20). Such is the loving, forgiving nature of God. The moment we repent (change our way of thinking), the Father runs to meet us and life begins to take on a new and brighter aspect.

The chapter concludes by stating that the rest of humankind, that is, those who had not the seal of God upon their foreheads and yet had survived the plagues, continued to go about their business as usual—unthinking, unrepentant. They continued in their materialistic way of worshiping demons (false and mischievous beliefs) and idols of gold and silver (worldly success and power) and living their grossly self-centered lives. Presumably, they also continued to live in the half light of materiality and sensuality, and to suffer from intermittent plagues. Such is the lot of unregenerate humanity!

The Sure Medicine

Revelation 10

Chapter ten opens with the appearance of another mighty angel of very imposing appearance, wrapped in a cloud, having a rainbow over his head, a face like the sun, and legs like pillars of fire. He stood with his right foot on the sea and his left foot on the land. Clearly this messenger was the bearer of good news, signified by the rainbow and the sunlike countenance, while the presence of the cloud and his ability to stand on both earth and sea indicated his authority over all conditions. He held a scroll, and after the sound of seven thunders he announced that there should be no more delay, that the mystery of God should be fulfilled.

John was then instructed, "Go, take the

scroll which is open in the hand of the angel"
(Rev. 10:8). John obeyed, and was then told,
"Take it and eat; it will be bitter to your
stomach, but sweet as honey in your mouth"
(Rev. 10:9). John did as ordered, and found it
was, indeed, sweet as honey to the taste, but
his stomach was made bitter. This truly is the
fulfilling of the mystery of God, the revealing
of the secret of the bittersweet happiness
that is God's goodwill for us all. This message—to know that we can be free and happy,
and have all our needs opulently, abundantly
met—is as sweet as honey; it is music to our
ears. But there is a cost. It tastes good, it
sounds good, but when we come to the point
of digestion, we find that it can be painful.
Truth can be hard to assimilate.

This analogy is highly appropriate. Truth
is much like a sugarcoated pill. We understand that by living with Truth principles we
can find our way from frustration to a sense
of purpose, from sickness to health, from inharmony to love, from lack to unlimited supply. We can be inspired by the examples set
by others who have made overcomings. We
can be uplifted and encouraged by helpful
books and lectures. But the time comes when
we must do what is necessary to make Truth
work in our own lives, and this frequently can

be a bitter experience. Jesus was emphatic on this point: "If any man would come after me, let him deny himself and take up his cross and follow me" (Mt. 16:24). We have to do the work ourselves; no one is going to do it for us!

Too often people are attracted by Truth teachings because they seek the healing of a condition, circumstance, or relationship, not realizing that both the cause of the malaise and its cure rest within themselves. They are looking for someone or something on the outside to heal them, but their healing lies in a change in their consciousness. Only deep and radical change in their way of thinking, attitudes, and behavior can result in a different life experience. The unspoken cry is, "Heal me, but do not ask me to change. I like me the way I am. Do not ask me to give up my habitual way of thinking, my anger, resentments, criticisms, and prejudices. Change the other person, change the outer conditions, but do not ask me to change." It does not work that way.

People do find healing of mind, body, relationships, and financial conditions through coming into Truth, but not as a result of seeking these as ends in themselves. These desirable outcomes are the result of "seeking first the kingdom." They come as a result of working with spiritual law and gaining spiritual understanding. Truth churches frequently offer courses in spiritual healing, prosperity, and right relationships, but these are peripheral to their main thrust of teaching the truth of humankind as being one with their creator, God. Unity churches teach wholeness—the oneness of humankind with God by virtue of the inner presence of the Christ, the I AM. They teach spiritual law—the laws of love, of cause and effect, of giving and receiving. They teach the power of the spoken word. The courses in such apparently specific subjects as healing and prosperity, for example, are but individual applications of Truth principles designed to recondition the subconscious mind, but always against the backdrop of the need to acquire spiritual understanding. The specific healing then follows as a matter of course, to the degree that consciousness is changed.

We recognize that healing is an outer manifestation of wholeness. The words *whole* and *holy* come from the same root. To be whole in body, we must first be holy in mind and in attitude. Health of body is often evidence of a healthy attitude, and of truly Godlike ways of thinking, speaking, and acting. The promise of good health is as sweet as honey, but finding health involves assimilating the pill of consciously changing our thinking, controlling our emotions, and being different in outlook and behavior.

Whatever the condition of our body, the truth is, we will not be completely well as long as we hold uncharitable and unloving thoughts about ourselves or others. Negative thinking about anyone or anything is injurious to one's own health. Pessimism and self-pity are slow suicide. Fear of disease lowers resistance to disease and, in fact, may attract it. Hostile and destructive thoughts promote the rapid destruction of one's own body cells. These are some examples of the ways in which our customary thinking can directly affect our physical health. But the average person is loathe to give up resentments, anger, and self-pity, saying, "I cannot forgive. I have been hurt too much." Yet change his thinking he must, if he is to find health.

Some people become so attached to the compensations of sickness that it would amount to bitter deprivation to give them up. Such compensations include the care and solicitude lavished on them by loved ones, the attention and sympathy they receive from others, and the freedom from responsibility and the burdens of normal living which they enjoy. Some find the cost of giving these up too great to contemplate. The pain would be "bitter in the stomach."

Similarly, with the meeting of our material needs the idea of access to the unlimited providence and supply of God is sweet to the taste, but the practical and mental steps necessary to attain this very desirable condition can be difficult and indeed painful for many people. The law of giving and receiving requires that we first give in order to receive, but some are reluctant to step out on faith and give to others for fear that they will be deprived as a result. The teaching of tithing one-tenth of one's income to the channel that meets one's spiritual needs often causes people to say, "I cannot afford to tithe," whereas in truth, their existing poverty should show them that they cannot afford not to tithe. Tithing is the proven method of attaining financial independence.

There is a universal cry for peace. The mystic Thomas à Kempis wrote: "All men desire peace, but few men do the things that make for peace." Peace will come when the peoples of the world desire peace in their innermost hearts to such an extent that they do the things that make for peace. Peace can be experienced by the individual who truly relinquishes the sources of unrest and disaffection within his own consciousness. An American Indian is alleged to have commented, "Many men smoke the peace pipe, but few men inhale." The idea of peace is sweet, but it can be too bitter an experience to give up resentments and antagonism.

After he had eaten the scroll, John was told, "You must again prophesy about many peoples and nations and tongues and kings" (Rev. 10:11). In other words, remind yourself and others that the Way will not always be sweetness and light. Surely, enough has now been said to bring us to the realization that, however sweet the fruits of living the Christ Way can be, to many people it would be too bitter a pill to swallow for them to relinquish their long established destructive tendencies. But for the committed follower of the Way, it is vital that the cost be faced and the medicine be taken. When difficulties arise and the bitterness of personal change is actually experienced, one may be tempted to give up, but the message of The Revelation to John is for us to persist to the end. There is no turning back. In the next chapter, the way of overcoming is revealed.

The Power of Optimism

Revelation 11

Concealed in chapter eleven is one of the most important secrets of triumphant and successful living. This secret is that we have available to us certain mental and spiritual qualities which, if called upon, will allow us to overcome all the frustrations and challenges that face us in life. This is as true for our daily living as it is for our spiritual development.

The chapter opens with John being instructed: "Rise and measure the temple of God and the altar and those who worship there, but do not measure the court outside the temple; leave that out, for it is given over to the nations, and they will trample over the holy city for forty-two months. And I will grant my two witnesses power to prophesy for one thousand two hundred and sixty days, clothed in sackcloth" (Rev. 11:1-3). These two witnesses are then likened to the two olive trees and the two lampstands which stand before the Lord of the earth.

It is again appropriate to remind ourselves of the nature of our study. The Revelation to John is a survival handbook for those who are on the spiritual path; its primary purpose is to encourage spiritual wayfarers to persist in their efforts to attain spiritual growth. All the incidents are to be seen as taking place within the consciousness of the spiritually aware individual. At the same time, we must remind ourselves that as wayfarers we are still *in* the world, while not necessarily being *of* the world. Revelation was not written only for the follower of the monastic life, but was also, and perhaps chiefly, intended for those who live in this contemporary world.

The message of Jesus Christ was addressed to the average person of His day, not the recluse. He came to help the ordinary man and woman of His or any time who had to contend with the problems that arise from being human—growing up, earning a living, finding a mate, raising a family, living with neighbors, working and providing employment. Life is for living, not something from which to escape. Humankind has the divinely ordained purpose of assisting civilization as it evolves to a point that, humanly, we are as yet unable to discern. There is within every human being the ability to observe his or her condition and want something different, something better. Every person has desires and ambitions. This comes as a result of the prompting of the I AM.

Humankind, therefore, has goals, plans for the immediate future, and also hopes for the long term. These goals doubtless vary from the material to the highest spiritual aspiration of ultimately attaining conscious oneness with God. Attainment of these goals is necessary for the spiritual health of the individual, for it is written, "Hope deferred makes the heart sick, but a desire fulfilled is a tree of life" (Prov. 13:12). Wherever the aspirant may be on the road of spiritual development, certain qualities are necessary to move from one stage to the next. This chapter contains the secret of attainment.

We recall that John was instructed to measure the temple of God and the altar, but to ignore the outer court. We have no difficulty in identifying the temple of God and the altar as being the mind of the individual when in the spiritual consciousness. We are told to measure it and its occupants. In other words, we are to devote our full attention to ensuring that the things we desire are in line with our spiritual goals, and that we use spiritual methods to attain these desires.

To fulfill these conditions we must first check our desires with the nature of the Lamb. Is that which we want loving, kind, compassionate? Have we ensured that its fulfillment will not result in harm to others? Further, we must do all we can to sustain the desire by using our creative imagination to see it fulfilled, and to nourish it with positive, affirmative thoughts that have been cleansed of all doubt or fear. The instruction to ignore the outer court should be heeded at all costs, for it is here that the existing appearances have had their way for so long. The nations—the world of "facts" and so-called "reality," all the human reasons why our longed-for prayer should not be granted—have trampled over the holy city for *forty-two months*, a biblical symbol for *a very long time*.

Now it is recommended that the eleventh chapter of The Revelation to John be reread in its entirety. In summary, two witnesses appear who are likened to olive trees and lampstands and they prophesy for one thousand two hundred and sixty days. They are promised divine protection. Nevertheless, the beast that ascends from the bottomless pit kills them and they lie unburied for three and one-half days. After this, God breathes the breath of life into them and they are restored and ascend into heaven, where there is great rejoicing.

Identification of the two witnesses provides us with a fascinating opportunity to prayerfully explore Bible meaning. Clearly, they must be spiritual elements that reveal the nature of the Lamb, yet also can seemingly be killed or conquered by negative events of life, while still possessing the unique property of being able to resurrect. At once we think of faith and hope, of good intentions and positive attitudes. Expressed another way, these would be good (Christlike) intentions, and belief in an outcome that is ultimately good or, in a single word, optimism.

It seems to be the nature of life that from time to time we experience setbacks and disappointments, that our plans are killed, our health suffers, or our happiness is destroyed. But this is not the end. Our hope for happiness, our faith in God, our good intentions combine to rekindle a positive and optimistic attitude. This frame of mind allows us to continue through seeming disaster. We rise again, ultimately to succeed. This time we are victorious, and inwardly we exult. We've made it. Our hopes were justified; our dreams came true. In consciousness, we are in heaven.

The details of the narrative comprise a fascinating example of storytelling. We are told that our attention should be concentrated on the temple and the altar. In other words, we should allow our minds to dwell on that which we desire, the object of our prayers and, at all costs, to ignore the outer court, or the appearance of lack, inharmony, or whatever it is that we wish to see replaced or improved. Concentrate on the objective and exclude all consideration of the possibility of failure or disappointment.

For "forty-two months" we have been aware of some need in our life. For all this period we have been conscious of our desire for change, but the nations of the world seem to have trampled our hopes, preventing us from attaining our desire. Then we read that the witnesses, faith and hope, albeit wearing sackcloth, have been bearing their testimony for three and one-half years, in other words, for an equal period! The message here is that however long the demonstration is deferred the witnesses, hope and faith, are equal to it.

The optimistic attitude can outlast disappointment.

We note that the enemy, the beast that appears to kill our dream, derives from the bottomless pit; in other words, there is no real or substantial reason for our not attaining our desires. This beast is the belief in error or negation that springs from our own fears, hesitation, and negativeness. But all these fears are groundless. There is no truth or permanence to the beast, and any power that it may seem to have is derived solely from our belief in it. It can assume terrifying proportions, and for a time it can slay our good intentions. But the unconquerable spirit of the Lamb will resuscitate faith and hope, and after an interval of only "three and a half days" (as compared to the three and a half years in which they witnessed), the demonstration will be attained.

The beauty of the fourth verse is worthy of special consideration. "These [two witnesses] are the two olive trees and the two lampstands which stand before the Lord of the earth" (Rev. 11:4). The two olive trees symbolize the oil of joy and peace and harmony. Throughout the waiting period let us rest in confident peace and not be resentful of delays or seeming obstacles; let us be joyous in the sure knowledge that our prayers are already answered in Spirit and must and will come into fruition. And the presence of the two lampstands ensures an abundance of light. There can be no darkness and we can go forward with sureness.

"They stand before the Lord of the earth." The Lord is that which governs. So we should make these two witnesses, faith and hope (the attitude of optimism), be the law for us. Our outlook on life should be unfailingly peaceful, joyous, confident, and optimistic. Paul told us, "So faith, hope, love abide" (1 Cor. 13:13). As we seek to live the fulfilled life, all these spiritual qualities are necessary. We must love our dream enough to protect it by having continuing faith and hope to nurture it, in spite of all the attacks of negation. "Faith is the assurance of things hoped for, the conviction of things not seen" (Heb. 11:1).

Underlying this tremendous lesson is immutable law. Mind is creative; the universe is affirmative in its action. Just as the manifest universe came into being following the affirmative action of Mind as recorded in the first chapter of Genesis, so our world comes into being in accordance with the predominating concepts we hold in mind. In a word, the universe always says "Yes." Our part is to maintain a hopeful, confident, positive attitude, and ultimately our prayers will be answered.

With this, we are told in the fourteenth verse that we have reached the end of the second woe. As we look back to chapter nine, verse twelve, and reread the intervening passages, we realize that this woe has painfully affected those who have resisted entering the consciousness of the Lamb, but the adherents of the Lamb have been spared. Once again the chapter concludes on a note of praise and worship as all those in heaven rejoice in thanksgiving for this latest triumph of the Christ. Again, this is the spontaneous paean of thanksgiving experienced in the consciousness of the wayfarer who, in the figurative sense, has ascended to heaven in a cloud. He is on "cloud nine."

You Can Win

Revelation 12

The ability of the power of faith and hope to produce answers in our lives when in the consciousness of the Lamb is repeated in the twelfth chapter, but this time a different and more telling image is presented. The wealth of detail and the penetrating ideas put forward in the symbolism should make the importance of the message inescapable. The introduction of the two witnesses establishes the principle that prayer, when supported by faith and hope, will bring desired good into our lives. The twelfth chapter illustrates the principle in action, but it also emphasizes the recurring and destructive menace that self-doubt and the harboring of evil thoughts can be.

It is recommended that the chapter be read in its entirety. Summarizing the early verses, we are told that a great portent appeared in heaven. A woman clothed with the sun and wearing a crown of stars is pregnant and, in travail, she cries out to be delivered. But a great red dragon appears and waits to devour the child. The child, a boy, is born and is safely carried up to God on His throne.

This time the central figure is a woman, representing both the creativity and the feeling nature of every individual. She is pregnant, and the fact that she is described as being clothed with the sun, having the moon at her feet, and wearing a crown of stars indicates that she is aware that she has conceived something of tremendous value to her. She is possessed by an idea of something immeasurably better than her existing experience. She is radiant with the joyous possibilities of the concept. In her mind's eye, she is already jubilantly enjoying the fulfillment of her dream. She is seeking to bring into being a new, rich, and higher experience.

But she is in travail; the birth pangs are extremely painful. Indeed, it hurts to change, and if we are to bring forth a new life, we must be willing to give up the old way of thinking. This calls for separation from the old. Travail has been described as being useful but necessary suffering. Suffering that is brought on by attempting to work against spiritual law is unnecessary, and could be avoided. But when we are seeking to break with an old, ingrained condition and create a new life, necessary suffering must be endured if we are to bring about the desired new condition. It is painful to exercise atrophied muscles, but in order to regain strength and flexibility, pain must be endured. One may seek to be free from addiction to tobacco, alcohol, or drugs, and the pangs of withdrawal can be agonizing, but to obtain freedom one must live through them. Similarly, in our efforts to grow spiritually we have realized that we must be more tolerant, compassionate, generous, forgiving, and understanding, and be willing to spend time contemplating the wonders and glories of God. The "old me" does not want to give the love, the caring, or the attention necessary, but we must do so if we are to grow. So we suffer! And this is probably true of achieving anything worthwhile that involves change, for to attain our heart's desire, we may suffer and may cry out in pain.

In the meantime, the great red dragon with "seven heads and ten horns" is waiting to devour the child. Charles Fillmore says this fearsome creature "means the personal or mortal self, and the seven heads are the seven ruling desires of this self. The ten horns are the five intellectual faculties doubled, because every faculty is dual and at war with itself." In order to deal effectively with this menace, it is vital that we understand the symbolism presented. The dragon, representing the personal or mortal self, is the very human level of our awareness while we are still in an unregenerate state. It is the ego while still in the subhuman condition. It is the physical and material consciousness that was so important in enabling us to climb out of the cave, but which we are now seeking to outgrow. This is the "me first" mentality, that level which believes that "might is right," that one must get ahead at all costs, even at the expense of another. It is basically selfish and antisocial, the reverse of the sublime condition of the Lamb, and it sees that to live the Way of the Lamb will result in its own eclipse.

This personal or mortal self is represented as having seven heads, which are the seven ruling desires of this self. Traditional Christianity has identified seven deadly, or cardinal, sins. These are anger, lust, sloth, covetousness, gluttony, pride, and envy. These may or may not be precisely those that were being shown to John, but suffice it to say they are certainly representative of the ruling passions that possess many people in their unregenerate state. Any one of these can be a threat to followers of the Way, and we are wise to be constantly on the watch, for each head has a mouth that is capable of devouring the unwary!

Then we learned that the dragon had ten horns, which represent "the five intellectual faculties doubled, because every faculty is dual and at war with itself." Let us equate these with the five senses of humankind: hearing, sight, smell, taste, and touch. We should remember that horns are not merely decorative, but possess the power to inflict wounds, perhaps fatal ones! Our senses are avenues of information from the outer world to our minds. It was intended that these should convey good information; however, they have now taken on the guise of horns and are capable of inflicting great harm, for they are now represented as being avenues of distortion or misinformation.

Our hearing becomes selective, and we, interested in hearing only that which is unhelpful and damaging, gossipy or critical, eagerly seek to hear that which is negative and derogatory; we find ourselves repeating lies and gossip for others to hear. Similarly with our sight, we develop a tendency to see only that which is negative and evil; we look for the error in every situation; we become picky and hypercritical. Our faculty to smell takes on a new twist and we find ourselves becoming unduly suspicious; we say, "I smell a rat," or, "There is something fishy here." Our taste may become selective in a negative way. In meeting others, we increasingly find situations becoming "distasteful," we become increasingly intolerant, things and people are no longer "to our taste"; they become repugnant to us. And finally, we become oversensitive, we are touchy, "thin-skinned," and quick to take offense. All these antisocial states of mind are destructive to our thinking, our attitudes, and our life experience. Our manifest life is bound to reflect the critical, hostile, and suspicious content of our minds, and life becomes hell.

So the dragon symbolizes humankind at our worst, our own fears, doubts, uncertainties, poor self-image, sense of unworthiness—in fact, everything in our consciousness that prompts us to question whether it will ever be possible for us to achieve the longed-for demonstration. Also, the dragon represents our unregenerate, critical, selfish outlook that is bound to bring only like effects into our lives. These threaten to kill off the new experience for which we long.

Already the power of the great red dragon has been exhibited, for "His tail swept down a third of the stars of heaven, and cast them to the earth" (Rev. 12:4). Charles Fillmore tells us stars represent "the inner conviction of our ability to accomplish whatever we undertake." So devastating are the doubts that can assail us that if we listen to them a significant part of our belief in ourselves (one-third of the stars in our personal heaven) will be destroyed.

But our precious idea is divinely protected. The child is born, the dragon is thwarted, and the male child is snatched up to heaven. This image is an echo of a bygone age when the highest ambition of a woman was to present her husband with a male child. It is representative of our own highest aspirations, our own deepest desires. This is a restatement of the promise that if we will do our part, God will do His. If we will endure the pain of change, and persist in spite of our own inadequacies, then in a seemingly miraculous way, divine intervention will occur.

The biblical account states, "She brought forth a male child, one who is to rule all the nations with a rod of iron" (Rev. 12:5). This is the new you. This is the new birth of which Jesus spoke, "Truly, truly, I say to you, unless one is born anew, he cannot see the kingdom of God" (Jn. 3:3). When we have made the changes in our thinking and attitudes to bring them in line with those of the Lamb, we will be able to rule our previously wayward thoughts, feelings, and emotions and truly take conscious control over our lives. We will have discovered and released the "imprisoned splendor" of which Browning wrote in "Paracelsus." The woman—the creative, feeling aspect of consciousness—then goes to the "wilderness, where she has a place prepared by God, in which to be nourished for one thousand two hundred and sixty days" (Rev. 12:6). This is the same length of time that the witnesses prophesied. This is the period of contemplation in solitude and physical inactivity where one continues to dwell in faith and hope.

Verses seven onward give an account of the war that arose in heaven. Even after apparently having brought into manifestation the desire that we have so longed for, there can remain in one's mind traces of incredulity

over having indeed achieved that which we
sought, or that we will be allowed to keep it.
These doubts must be dealt with resolutely.
We are told that Michael and his angels
fought against the dragon and his angels, and
were victorious. Michael stands for divine inspiration, the realization of the all-conquering
power of God. To receive this inspiration and
to come into the realization of God's all-
conquering power, we must be faithful in
spending time in the silence, be receptive to
that inspiration, and declare God's invincibil-
ity until it has become an integral part of our
being. Do this, and again we have the assurance that the angelic hosts will be on our side
as long as we persist. The defeated dragon is
thrown down to earth.

As this occurs, it is revealed that the great
dragon and "that ancient serpent, who is
called the Devil and Satan, the deceiver of the
whole world" (Rev. 12:9), are one and the
same! "The ancient serpent" provoked
humans to fall from their Edenic state of see-
ing only good in the world, by tempting them
to eat of the tree of the knowledge of good
and evil. By so doing, they "died" to the
awareness of rich and joyous living. Jesus,
speaking of the devil, called him "a liar and
the father of lies" (Jn. 8:44). The devil does

not exist as an entity in Truth. He is a lie; there is no truth in him.

The Truth is, there is only one Presence and one Power in the universe, God the good, Omnipotent. There is no entity that is basically evil, at war with God and His forces for good; there is only God. But humankind has been given the formative power of thought, and we introduce evil into our own lives by belief in our own evil imaginings. The devil is the totality of the miscreations abroad in the race mind—the race consciousness of negation that must be reckoned with. The dragon has been "thrown down to the earth" (Rev. 12:9). Now we face negation in the practical affairs of life. Now the new birth must be proved, and we are confronted by the challenge of showing forth our new way of thinking in daily life and in the marketplace.

John then reports that he heard a loud voice in heaven announcing that "the salvation and the power and the kingdom of our God and the authority of his Christ have come" (Rev. 12:10), and that the accuser had been brought down "by the blood of the Lamb" (Rev. 12:11). Read verses ten through twelve. The dragon has been wounded and cast down, but he is not yet terminally vanquished. He continues to reappear in one form or another, and it is only "the blood of the Lamb" that can effectively conquer him. At the risk of appearing repetitive, it is profitable for us to remind ourselves of what is involved in "the blood of the Lamb." "The blood of the Lamb" refers to that consciousness that is wholehearted in its worship of the one God and all that this implies: courage in facing up to one's own limitations and shortcomings, unfailing love and compassion in dealings with other people, and willingness to sacrifice all, to the point of death, to maintain principle; in other words, to be a dedicated disciple of the Jesus Christ teachings in every area of life. As we seek to attain and maintain this consciousness, many of the sufferings that are described in this and later chapters will be avoided.

The great red dragon has been vanquished and cast down to earth. Persistently he pursues the woman, but she has fled to the safety of the wilderness. In the wilderness there is solitude, quiet, peace. In quiet reflection she can renew her realization of oneness with God, All-Good. Here the woman discovers the power of affirmation. She flies "to the place where she is to be nourished for a time, and times, and half a time" (Rev. 12:14). This statement can be interpreted as a reference to the necessity for working with statements of Truth long enough that they have become thoroughly embedded in the mind. The most effective time for such a practice is just before going to sleep. One compiles a statement of Truth and speaks it, then repeats it time after time after time until one falls asleep in the middle of the repetition. In the Scriptures, "a time, and times, and half a time" translates as three and one-half years. The dragon has no effective response to this treatment and departs, "to make war on the rest of her offspring" (Rev. 12:17).

Choose You This Day

Revelation 13

Chapter thirteen opens with John observing a beast rising out of the sea. This beast has certain characteristics in common with the great red dragon who dominated the previous chapter, having ten horns and seven heads, with the addition of having a blasphemous name on its seven heads. Also, it "was like a leopard, its feet were like a bear's, and its mouth was like a lion's mouth" (Rev. 13:2). The added details of the makeup of the beast convey the impression of a stealthy, cruel, and predatory creature of great ferocity and unlimited appetite, capable of inflicting disabling, possibly fatal damage.

We discussed the metaphysical meaning of the seven heads and the ten horns in the previous chapter. Now in the light of the evil characteristics of this new beast, we are wise to reflect on the nature of its two added peculiarities. These are, first, that it had "a blasphemous name upon its heads" (Rev. 13:1), and second, that "one of its heads seemed to have a mortal wound, but its mortal wound was healed" (Rev. 13:3).

The presence of the blasphemous name indicates the habitual misuse of the name of God, or using the name of God in a derogatory manner. Again, it should be recalled that we are dealing with the consciousness of the individual. God's name, He told us, is I AM. Our use of the term "I am" not merely has the effect of identifying ourselves, but of using the power of God's name to identify with a condition. This is true whether it be done consciously or unconsciously, that is, deliberately or unthinkingly. It will at once be realized that the individual in the consciousness of any of the dragon's seven heads—angry, lustful, proud, covetous, slothful, gluttonous, or envious—or in the mood of any of the ten horns—critical, hostile, suspicious, resentful, and quick to take offense, and who is full of self-doubt and negative imaginings—can suffer terrible injury and torment from this beast.

Add to this the fact that it is capable of recovery from what appeared to be a mortal wound inflicted in a previous bout, and this new beast is indeed a redoubtable foe, one to be greatly respected as an adversary.

We are then told that men worshiped both the dragon and the beast, that the dragon vested all its authority in the beast, and also that the beast was allowed to exercise its authority for forty-two months, and to "make war on the saints and to conquer them" (Rev. 13:7). Men "worshiped the beast, saying, 'Who is like the beast, and who can fight against it?' " (Rev. 13:4) The previous chapter concluded with the dragon going off to make war on the rest of the woman's offspring, and those who keep the commandments of God and bear testimony to Jesus. It would have seemed that with the dragon being thrown down to earth, he was vanquished. But no. Essentially he has reappeared, healed from his previous encounter, but now in a new and more dangerous guise.* Humankind is not capable of remaining for a long period of time in the high state of con-

---

*Editor's note: Traditionally the "beast with mortal wound . . . healed" referred to Nero. Myth had it that he did not die and would return.

sciousness that puts him beyond the reach of the great dragon. He must remain constantly vigilant. In this chapter we are being warned in metaphysical terms of the dangers that continue to confront us on the spiritual path even after we have made a deep commitment. We have to live *in* the world. Our need is to ensure that we are not *of* the world.

The pressures of materiality are great and ever present. It is not easy to maintain one's own code while living satisfactorily with people who have not made a commitment to live the Way of the Lamb. The temptation to lower one's standards in order to conform to the mores of society is strong. Men worshiped the beast, and "Who can fight against it?" In every area of life there seem to be compelling reasons for trimming one's sails in order to catch a favorable breeze that would appear to give one some advantage, but the spiritual cost is great.

The fact that the beast is pictured as having ten horns symbolizes the multiple ways in which the "devil" is able to impale and wound. Most people faithfully observe the majority of the Christian and ethical teachings, yet it is probably also true to say that many people are vulnerable to temptation in one or more areas. It is in those particularly sensitive areas that the attack occurs.

Note that the beast was allowed to make war on and conquer the saints for a period of only forty-two months, or the same period that the nations were allowed to trample over the outer court of the temple (see Rev. 11:2). But it was for an equal length of time (one thousand two hundred and sixty days) that the two witnesses, faith and hope, were prophesying, although clothed in sackcloth. To be "clothed in sackcloth" indicates grief, regret, remorse. The "saints" did not like themselves; they knew they had done wrong in some area and their consciences were making them miserable. The beast had "killed" them, and they lay unburied for three and a half days, when "a breath of life from God entered them, and they stood up on their feet, and . . . . they went up to heaven in a cloud" (Rev. 11:11-12). This "breath of life" is the determination to change.

This is the assurance to dedicated followers of the Way. While still in the world we doubtless will be subject to many attacks from the beast, promising shortcuts and easier ways to obtain happiness and satisfaction, but if these are not in conformity with the Way approved by the Lamb, disappointment, pain, and remorse await. If we allow faith and hope to bear witness, the breath of God will enter, bringing redemption.

The proof of the efficacy of this spiritual principle was dramatically illustrated for me by the experience of a man who came to me for counsel. He was not a Truth student but was attracted to our philosophy by our radio messages. So deep was his trouble that he would not give me his name. He told me that he was a good churchgoer and occupied a position of trust in which he managed other people's funds. He had made a very bad investment, which had resulted in his incurring a severe personal financial loss. His wife was passing through a grave illness, which had drained his resources, and he had "borrowed" funds from the account of one of his clients. The shortage in the account might not be discovered for years, by which time he hoped to make it good. On the other hand, he was desperately afraid that there might be an accounting at any time. Now his conscience bothered him. He was haunted by the fear of discovery, prosecution, and imprisonment. What should he do?

We talked about various possibilities; then, at my suggestion, we prayed together for guidance and went into a time of silence, during which he was to ask God what he ought to do. When we emerged and I asked him what he felt he ought to do, he responded at once that he had no doubt that he ought to confess his mistake to his client, but that he had been praying for some other way—how could he get hold of that much money to put it back? Should he run away and lose himself? Suicide? I then discussed with him the inner meaning of Psalms twenty-seven; if he would follow the way of the Lord, he need have no fear because the Lord would be his light and his salvation. The Lord, his Lord, had said in essence, "Go and confess, and I will save you."

But the man protested. "That is suicide. This guy will eat me. He will call the police and throw me into jail. He's tough. You don't know these business types!" I told him the promise would stand. If he would follow the directions of the Christ, the Lord would see him through. Whatever happened it would be the best in the long run. The Christ had given him light, in the form of direction. The Christ would give him strength to see it through, and the Christ would also give him salvation. He would be saved. If he would "wait on the Lord," that is, persist in prayer and meditation, he would be given the strength to do what he had to do. He was quiet, and finally left without having made a decision.

He came to see me about three weeks later. He had tried to forget the whole matter, but it wouldn't go away. The fear of discovery haunted him and he had finally decided that confession was the lesser evil. He had finally mustered up his courage, asked for an appointment with the client, and blurted out what he had done. He said his client was shocked, angry, and abusive, but had eventually calmed down. At length he had said, "If I report you, you'll be jailed, and I'll never get my money. So you sign a note to pay me back by installments. But if you default, I'll blow the whistle on you." The man told me that now he felt happy and relieved. He said he had been reading Psalms twenty-seven, and he felt just like the psalmist in the sixth verse, who writes, "And now my head shall be lifted up above my enemies round about me . . . I will sing and make melody to the Lord." In a symbolic way, he "went up to heaven in a cloud" as the witnesses in The Revelation to John had done.

Chapter thirteen contains a clear warning of the necessity for vigilance, for the beast was given authority "over every tribe and people and tongue and nation, and all . . . whose name has not been written . . . in the book of life of the Lamb" (Rev. 13:7-8). Then follows a restatement of the law of cause and effect: "If any one is to be taken [that is, takes another] captive, to captivity he goes; if any one slays with the sword, with the sword must he be slain" (Rev. 13:10). Only by staying close to the Way of the Lamb are we protected from the machinations of this beast, for as we break spiritual law so shall we surely be called on for an accounting.

The subtlety of the methods of the liar devil is further illustrated in the eleventh verse of this chapter, when we are told that another beast rose out of the earth: "It had two horns like a lamb and it spoke like a dragon" (Rev. 13:11). This beast was superficially "like a lamb" and was able to work great signs. Yet it had all the nature and authority of both the dragon and the first beast and deceived those who dwell on earth; that is, those who are in the material consciousness.

We note that this beast had two horns and looked like a lamb. The word *lamb* as used here is not capitalized, as in the case of the Lamb whose spirit we seek to emulate. However, the fact that this beast is like a lamb in appearance indicates that it was intended to be mistaken for the Lamb by the unwary. But the presence of the two horns warns us of its potential for injury. The two horns represent *intolerance* and *self-righteousness*. These unpleasant characteristics typify the pseudo-spiritual person who is nevertheless still steeped in the ways of the world. Such people may be found in many churches and religious groups—strict adherents to the letter of the law of their belief, but wholly devoid of any of the saving graces that make up the true Christian, such as love, understanding, and compassion. These people are of the nature of the first beast—ferocious, predatory, and merciless—and speak like the dragon—domineering, materialistic, and grasping—yet wear the trappings of religion. It was the mindset of the second beast that produced the Inquisition and Puritanism, and other aberrations that may come to mind. Again, the earmarks are intolerance and self-righteousness.

In this chapter we are told that men worshiped the dragon and the beast, and the second beast not merely encouraged this, but caused to be slain those who refused. The second beast also was able to work great signs and achieve much worldly success. In chapter sixteen this second beast is referred to as the false prophet. The follower of the Way must of necessity be vigilant lest he fall into the trap of following the teachings of the second beast and find himself unwittingly worshiping the dragon, or Antichrist.

Again, the purpose of this study is to relate these great truths to the spiritual progress of individuals. The inherent danger is not so much that we might find ourselves the victims of other people as it is that we, ourselves, might exhibit these tendencies. Intolerance and self-righteousness will wreak incalculable damage to our consciousness and delay our progress. Of course, should we mistakenly or unconsciously worship the dragon or the beast, we will find that these elements will ultimately rebound on us. This second beast appears to be benign, but it is nonetheless devastating in its influence.

The second beast causes all—small and great, rich and poor, free and slave—to bear the mark of 666 on his right hand or forehead. Six is half of twelve. Twelve symbolizes spiritual completion. One Unity School publication expresses it so: Six=half of twelve; Six=half of whole, not whole, un-whole, unholy. Thus 666 or six repeated three times could symbolize repeated attempts to negate the meaning of twelve or to negate spiritual wholeness. The mark of the beast was a badge of identification and was worn either on the right hand or the forehead. Metaphysically, this means that it would become evident from one's actions or by the way in which one thought that one either was or was not a worshiper of the beast. One either conformed to the actions and thinking of the herd, or one was peculiar, and as a result ostracized. As John somewhat wryly commented, "This calls for wisdom: let him who has understanding reckon" (Rev. 13:18) carefully which way he chooses.

Redeemed by the Lamb

Revelation 14

The chapter opens with the Lamb standing on Mount Zion with 144,000 of those who had his name and the Father's name written on their foreheads. Metaphysically, Mount Zion means love's abode where high, holy thoughts and ideals abide. From this group there emanated thunderous sounds of a new song, known only to the redeemed. This joyous group, described as being chaste and spotless, was singing before the throne. With them were the four living creatures and the elders.

This group of 144,000 is representative of those individuals who have followed the Lamb and have faithfully adhered to His Way. We discussed the number 144,000 in an earlier chapter and realized that this assembly is not limited to that precise number. This group is comprised of any and all individuals who are wholly dedicated in their way of thinking and behavior to living the life of Truth and thus are worthy to stand before the throne. In midheaven an angel is proclaiming an eternal gospel to all those who dwell on earth, "Fear God and give him glory, for the hour of his judgment has come" (Rev. 14:7).

These events are apparently proceeding at the same time that the events recorded in the previous chapter are taking place. From this we gather that while the second beast is having his way with the multitudes on earth (in the worldly consciousness), the followers of the Lamb are joyously standing before the throne, living in the light of love, surrounded by high and holy thoughts. Those in the worldly consciousness are still in the throes of the third woe. There is no reference in The Revelation to John to the third woe ever coming to an end. From this we must infer that woe will always be the lot of those who persist in ignoring the Way of the Lamb. Nevertheless, the opportunity of redemption is always being offered, for the eternal gospel is continually being proclaimed: "Fear God and give him glory, for the hour of his judgment has come." People are constantly being judged (judging themselves) by the sure results of their own actions. Divine judgment is always at work in every life.

To underline the folly of ignoring the Way of the Lamb, a second angel is saying, "Fallen, fallen is Babylon the great" (Rev. 14:8). In other words, the path of materialism is doomed to ultimate destruction. It may appear to hold sway for a time, apparently achieving great earthly importance and power, but eventually it must fall. Yet in the meantime, all its followers will be subject to the woes described.

A third angel predicts the dire effects that will be the lot of anyone who "worships the beast . . . he also shall drink the wine of God's wrath" (Rev. 14:9-10). This is not to be misunderstood as speaking of a vengeful and punitive God. Rather, it is an apt description of the way in which we must suffer mentally as long as any elements that are unlike the Christ remain in our makeup. Whenever we become aware of any tendency toward error, negativity, violence, or revenge, our conscience will torment us until we burn it away in the cleansing fire of Truth. We will truly "have no rest, day or night" (Rev. 14:11), until this is accomplished. Then Spirit aptly comments, "Here is a call for the endurance of the saints, those who keep the commandments of God and the faith of Jesus" (Rev. 14:12). In other words, continue in your faith and all those dire consequences will be avoided.

Then in verses thirteen through twenty there is a graphic restatement of the operation of the law of cause and effect in our experience. "Blessed are the dead who die in the Lord henceforth . . . that they may rest from their labors, for their deeds follow them!" (Rev. 14:13) Blessed are those who allow the past to remain in the past; they can rest in the realization that every good and positive thing they have done or attempted to do will remain with them. No good thing is lost. Then follow the angels with sickles, or the awareness that the time of harvest is always with us. "Put in your sickle, and reap, for the hour to reap has come" (Rev. 14:15). As we have sown, so shall we reap! The dramatic imagery of "the great wine press of the wrath of God" (Rev. 14:19) reiterates the unfailing operation of God's law of divine justice.

Armageddon

Revelation 15, 16, and 17

With these chapters, we have reached a crucial stage in the progress of the follower of the Way. By this time we have become aware of the great difference in the experiences of two types of people: the worshipers of the beast on the one hand, and the followers of the Lamb on the other. The great majority of people have been beguiled by the "liar and the father of lies" (Jn. 8:44), and are content to display the mark of the beast, and so be accepted by their contemporaries in society. The follower of the Way has come to realize that worshiping the beast is the road of continued "woes" and that eventually Babylon will fall. There is no future in it. The followers of the Lamb have had a glimpse of the transcendent joy that can be theirs as they are faithful and true.

However, there is no nice division between the two sets of people. In truth this dichotomy is present in the consciousness of all individuals, however far along the road of life they may be. This is not the story of "we and they"; it is all our own story. Within the consciousness of all, there is this continuing tug-of-war between the two ways of life. So the Comforter proceeds to illustrate the battle that is constantly going on in the spiritual life of the initiate.

Chapter fifteen opens with a great portent when seven angels appear with seven plagues. Also at this time, those who had resisted the blandishments of the beast are singing the song of Moses and the song of the Lamb. The song of Moses refers to the song of praise and thanksgiving that the Children of Israel sang upon being delivered from the Egyptians at the Red Sea (Ex. 15:1-18). Moses, of course, was also the great lawgiver. The basic law of the universe is that Mind is creative. This is true of both God-Mind and human mind. And Jesus, epitomized by the Lamb, gave us the new commandment of love. The resulting song was one of praise to the Lord God Almighty. This is the spontaneous outpouring from the heart of the dedicated follower of the Way.

However, as if to underline that we are not yet secure in our faith, the vision includes the appearance of seven angels (messengers from God) with plagues! The purpose of our being on this earth plane is to learn the lessons that life has to present to us. By this time we have reached that point in our unfoldment where our greatest desire is to come into the consciousness of our true oneness with God. "At the great heart of humanity there is a deep and awful homesickness that never has been and never can be satisfied with anything less than a clear, vivid consciousness of the indwelling presence of God, our Father" *(Lessons in Truth).* Therefore, within each of us there is the demand for growth, a need to be faced with the next steps in our spiritual unfoldment, challenging though these may be. These are presented by the seven angels.

It is not unusual, when some people are confronted by challenges of a harsh nature, to spend much time in introspection seeking to discover where they have seemingly broken the law. How did they attract this disaster? What was there in their awareness that produced this event? It can be a source of consolation to know that any seeming challenge is in reality a response to their own conscious or unconscious demand for growth. The best course is always to meet every seeming problem with the attitude of complete nonresistance and make the overcoming in consciousness. This counsel holds good for every seemingly difficult circumstance. Always, we have drawn it to us, and always the answer lies in attaining inner mastery.

One of the living creatures handed to each of the seven angels a golden bowl full of the wrath of God, and we were told "no one could enter the temple until the seven plagues of the seven angels were ended" (Rev. 15:8). This is a clear indication that we must persist in the task of cleansing our hearts and minds until it is complete. The alternative is too horrible to contemplate; it is to suffer from the plagues contained in the bowls. The first angel "poured his bowl on the earth, and foul and evil sores came upon the men who bore the mark of the beast" (Rev. 16:2). One by one, the remaining angels emptied their bowls. Although not expressly stated, it must be assumed that in each of the following cases it was also those "who bore the mark of the beast" who suffered the ill effects of the various plagues, and the followers of the

Lamb were immune.

Studying the various plagues, it would appear that the first afflicts the physical bodies of the individuals, causing them great personal suffering. The second, third, and fourth appear to be afflictions on the environment, causing humankind to have unspeakably miserable living conditions, while the fifth and sixth appear to relate to mental anguish and dementia arising from the misuse of mind. However, we should again remind ourselves that all these plagues do, indeed, exist in the mind of the individual. These are the very real appearing plagues that haunt people in the small hours, when conscience is robbing them of sleep, and fear and anxiety are holding sway.

Nevertheless, we well know the powerful effect of thought processes on the manifest life of the individual. The study of psychosomatic medicine confirms what Charles Fillmore and other metaphysicians have known for scores of years, that mental concepts have their way of becoming outpictured in the body and circumstances of individuals. This is to say that while the torture that worshipers of the beast endure is primarily in the mind, their bodies and circumstances must also inevitably suffer.

Of particular interest is the effect of empty-ing the bowl by the sixth angel. This resulted in there issuing from the mouths of the dragon, the beast, and the false prophet three foul spirits to "go abroad to the kings of the whole world, to assemble them for battle on the great day of God the Almighty. . . . at the place which is called in Hebrew Armaged-don" (Rev. 16:14-16). This is one of the passages that those who teach the inerrancy of the Bible believe is still to come to pass; that one day there will literally be a final armed conflict between the forces of good and evil, and then the millennium will arrive. For centuries people have been forecasting when Armageddon will be. Among a number of guesses that have been incorrect are the final battle between the Crusaders and the Sara-cens to liberate the Holy Land, the battle of Waterloo ending the Napoleonic wars, World War I, and then World War II; but still the millennium has not arrived! It does seem to be a little illogical to believe in the literal fulfillment of an isolated incident, when so many other elements in the book are clearly pure symbolism.

Armaggedon means "mountain of Megid-do." Megiddo was the site of at least two famous battles in Hebrew history. (See

Judges 5:19 and 2 Kings 23:29.)

In spite of the many conjectures as to when the "great day of God the Almighty" will be, we in Truth know that God Almighty is timeless, ageless, infinite, eternal, without beginning or end. In God there are no yesterdays, no tomorrows, there is only the eternal, ever-present now. Now is the great day of God the Almighty. Now is the day of decision. So the battle of Armageddon is proceeding now. Today is the day of decision! Today is judgment day!

Followers of the Way know well that this battle is fought within the consciousness of every individual. It is the struggle between negative impulses and aspirations to attain higher consciousness. Many people fight this conflict daily, perhaps several times a day.

Armageddon is the internal battle that every person is engaged in at some time or another. Sometimes it is conducted decisively and confidently, while at other times it can be a constant, indecisive, never-ending battle that destroys all the joy in a person's life. Everyone becomes aware of dissatisfaction with some area in life at some time and desires to be different, but along with this is the awareness of the difficulties in bringing about the desired change. Questions, doubts, and fears rush in, threatening to overwhelm the desired improvement. It is at this point that we need to bring in the full support of affirmative prayer and visualization, making a mental picture of the accomplished goal. This is seldom easy.

The truth about any situation is the fulfillment of your every good desire. You are a spiritual being, made in the image and after the likeness of your Creator, God. You are creative. Your thought was intended to be the tool to create conditions conforming to your good desires. But negation in the form of doubts about your own divinity creep in. Our part is to hold on in faith, knowing that the Lamb will defeat the forces of reaction and evil. Armageddon is that place and time in consciousness where the struggle takes place between the willingness to think the truth, and the concepts of negation.

At this crucial point the Comforter reminds us of the need to be on the alert. Parenthetically, we are told in chapter sixteen, verse fifteen, "Lo, I am coming like a thief! Blessed is he who is awake, keeping his garments that he may not go naked and be seen exposed!" The temptations to worship the beast and the pressures to follow the herd are very strong and not always easy to recognize, and may attack when least expected. So, "Put on the whole armor of God. . . . having girded your loins with truth . . . the breastplate of righteousness . . . the shield of faith" (Eph. 6:11-16).

The battleground is in our own minds. In the course of daily experience there may appear to be many reasons to be anxious, fearful, resentful, unforgiving, selfish, and acquisitive. But these emotions in turn produce additional actual events that will in their turn cause us more pain and loss, and so increase the fearful and unloving thoughts. For, again, the law is: What we think on grows! Our best course in the face of the temptation to compromise any standard is to recognize it at once for what it is—a trick—and to turn to the Christ indwelling and reaffirm our loyalty to the Lamb. It calls for nothing short of making a decision for Christ, and never wavering.

To the follower of the Way, the phrase "making a decision for Christ" means to be willing to follow the direction of the Christ in all things. It should be added that this is not making any narrow, sectarian call. The "Christ" is the name we give to the universal spirit of God individualized in every person. In essence it is a decision to accept as truth that this is a wholly good universe, and that we shape our lives by our thinking. So we decide to live and think positively, confidently, courageously, and lovingly, thus following the teachings of Jesus Christ.

Then the seventh angel poured his bowl into the air, and a great voice came from the temple saying, "It is done!" (Rev. 16:17) Amid a mighty storm and a great earthquake, the city of Babylon was made to drain the cup of the fury of God's wrath, and was split into three parts and destroyed. Scholars agree that Babylon in this passage is a cryptic reference to Rome. However, metaphysically, the city of Babylon represents the sensual, seductive, degenerative elements in the makeup of humankind. It represents negation and the utter emptiness and hollowness of materialism. It stands for vanity, confusion, and chaos. So the downfall of Babylon demonstrates the futility of worldliness and materiality.

Following the destruction of Babylon, the seat of materiality, John was then shown the fate of the harlot, a woman seated on a scarlet beast. She was arrayed in purple and scarlet and bedecked with jewels and pearls, holding a golden cup full of abominations. The beast will hate her and devour her flesh. The angel

then offers an explanation of the connection
between the woman and the beast that "was
and is not and is to come" (Rev. 17:8). It is
revealed that she and Babylon are one and
the same. The beast, we note, ascends from
the bottomless pit. In other words, it is
without foundation. From all this we gather
that evil is illusory, yet seems to have great
power and authority. This power is indicated
by the presence of the "ten kings" who "have
not yet received royal power" but receive
power for "one hour." In other words, their
power and authority have no real substance
and are temporary. They have only the power
vested in them by the belief of those whom
they have deceived, and the moment their
dupes resolutely decide to resist them, their
power vanishes. Babylon, the harlot, and the
beast are the products of "the deceiver" and
"father of lies," and none of them has any
true substance; they are illusory. But humankind, by its belief in and worship of these
deceivers, has constructed for itself elements
capable of causing untold unhappiness, pain,
and misery.

Armageddon, then, is that time and place
in consciousness when we, in full awareness
of the issues at stake, allow these forces for
evil within our own minds to be recognized

for the illusions they are, and "they will make war on the Lamb, and the Lamb will conquer them, for he is Lord of lords and King of kings, and those with him are called and chosen and faithful" (Rev. 17:14). In very simple terms, Armageddon is that place in consciousness where there is struggle between negativeness and our willingness to think Truth. The closing verses of the seventeenth chapter remind us that evil will eventually destroy itself, "for God had put it into their hearts to carry out his purpose" (Rev. 17:17).

Changing Values

Revelation 18

Chapter eighteen has a poignance and relevance that demand careful study by the follower of the Way. It opens with a statement by an angel speaking with great authority. This announcement reiterated the fall of Babylon (Rome) and recounted something of the depths of its depravity and the support it had received from the nations, the kings of the earth, and the merchants. This refers to the widespread acceptance of all that Babylon and Rome stood for among every level of the population, the people, the rulers, and the rich and successful. This indicates that we, too, whoever we are, must at some point have been included among the devotees of Babylon. There are no exceptions.

Then another voice, God's, speaks to the follower of the Way with a loving invitation, "Come out of her, my people, lest you take part in her sins, lest you share in her plagues" (Rev. 18:4). This is a timely reminder that although Babylon is fallen in spirit, it still exists in the minds and experience of those who worship it! Ultimately, Babylon is no more, but the overthrow of this wicked influence must be accomplished in the consciousness of every individual. Armageddon was not a one-time victory for the Lamb, but is an encounter that must be experienced time and again, as long as humankind exists. In an earlier chapter we discovered that the beast can suffer a "mortal" wound, yet still recover. So it is with Babylon; although overthrown, it is capable of being rebuilt in the minds of the unwary. The account of its fall is indeed valid for those who truly follow the Lamb and have "his Father's name written on their foreheads" (Rev. 14:1). But its overcoming has to be experienced in the consciousness of every individual growing soul.

Then follows a poignant account of various elements in our makeup as we mourn the destruction of Babylon, and the sense of deprivation we will experience. In spite of our aspiration for a higher and holier way of life, the familiar has its attractions, and there is that in us that regrets its departure and resists change. There would appear to be four separate areas of consciousness that are particularly affected and which make it especially difficult to give up the old way of thinking.

The first of these is referred to in verse nine, where it states "the kings of the earth, who committed fornication . . . will weep and wail" (Rev. 18:9). This has to do with those elements in us that long to dominate others, and may have misled others into following wrong and inappropriate courses. It has to do with ego, lack of humility, reliance on human and worldly standards, the discounting of spiritual values.

Verses eleven through fourteen contain a catalog of the so-called good things of life and "the merchants of the earth weep and mourn for her . . . " (Rev. 18:11), lamenting, "all thy dainties and thy splendor are lost" (Rev. 18:14). As we read this list we receive a distinct impression of self-indulgence, sensuality, privilege misused, sloth, and the enslavement of mind to evil.

Verse seventeen records the merchants of those wares wailing, "In one hour all this wealth has been laid waste." Such might well be the reaction of all who fail to trust God for the supply of their material needs, but who are consumed with greed, gluttony, envy, and covetousness.

Finally, the shipmasters and seafaring men wept and mourned: "Alas, alas, for the great city where all who had ships at sea grew rich" (Rev. 18:19). Their regret reflects the fear of want, the insecurity of those who are materialistic and without true spiritual foundation.

These human tendencies that we have had to uproot were perhaps once very necessary to our survival, as we made our long progress from our subhumanity on the way to the spiritual maturity that is our destiny. We have truly advanced out of the animal consciousness where the physical nature of the environment made such competitiveness an essential element in our continuing to live. Now we are entering a new era, and the elements that allowed us to continue to exist have become a hindrance and a drag on our progress. We must, at all costs, shed these tendencies. This knowledge that we are evolving out of a dark age into a new and brighter experience will assist us in overcoming. It may have been a wrench to give up all these so familiar ways of thinking, but as we do so, the spirit of God within us exults, "Rejoice over her, O heaven, O saints and apostles and prophets, for God

has given judgment for you against her!"
(Rev. 18:20)

Then, as if to re-emphasize the passing of
one standard of values to a new one, "a
mighty angel took up a stone like a great
millstone and threw it into the sea, saying,
'So shall Babylon the great city be thrown
down with violence, and shall be found no
more; and the sound of harpers and minstrels,
of flute players and trumpeters, shall be
heard in thee no more; and a craftsman of any
craft shall be found in thee no more' " (Rev.
18:21-22). This implies no criticism of music
and sundry skills. Rather, it tells us that
these will no longer satisfy, that in the new
era the things that we once thought to be
beautiful and fulfilling will pall into in-
significance, when compared to the things
that lie in store for us.

Help Is Available

Revelation 19 and 20

Chapter nineteen opens with a great song of jubilation and praise; this is the spontaneous emanation from the soul that has progressed thus far. "Hallelujah! Salvation and glory and power belong to our God" (Rev. 19:1). Joining us are all our spiritual resources; "And the twenty-four elders and the four living creatures fell down and worshiped God" (Rev. 19:4). All of our awakened spiritual nature unites in this heartfelt sense of rapture. It becomes even more joyous as we receive the inner invitation to the marriage supper with the Lamb. There is born in our consciousness the realization that at last we can establish conscious union with the Christ.

These are transcendent moments, and for a time we are tempted to seek these for themselves, when verse ten brings an abrupt admonition: "Then I fell down at his feet to worship him [the angel], but he said to me, 'You must not do that! . . . Worship God.' " We still have work to do in the manifest world, and we must not try to escape into a monastic retirement from life.

As if to prepare us for the events that are to follow, the white horse now reappears and his rider is called Faithful and True. This is the rider whom we met before in chapter six. On that occasion he was the first to emerge after the opening of the first seal, signifying that the spiritual element must always be given pre-eminence. We note that in righteousness he judges and makes war and that he is known by the name of "The Word of God." He is followed by the armies of heaven clad in the purest of white raiment and similarly mounted on white horses. This is a most heartening symbol. Hitherto, we may have felt that we were alone in fighting our battles against the forces of evil pictured variously as the dragon and the beasts and their minions. But no. We have but to call on the Word of God and immediately there will be unlimited spiritual resources available to us to make war on the negative elements and give us the victory.

There followed just such an engagement. The beast and the false prophet were supported by the forces of materiality and degeneracy gathered to make war on the Word of God, but they were utterly defeated (verses 19-21). "These two were thrown alive into the lake of fire that burns with sulphur" (Rev. 19:20). The fire represents cleansing, and this denotes that whatever evil was contained in that experience has been destroyed.

Chapter twenty opens with the appearance of an angel bearing the key to the bottomless pit and a great chain. "And he seized the dragon, that ancient serpent, who is the Devil and Satan, and bound him for a thousand years, and threw him into the pit, and shut it and sealed it . . . till the thousand years were ended. After that he must be loosed for a little while" (Rev. 20:2-3). We remember that Jesus had identified Satan as "a liar and the father of lies" (Jn. 8:44), and his home is the "bottomless pit." Thus there is no substance in this evil; it does not exist in Truth and its only power is that which has been vested in it by those whom it has deceived. That power, nevertheless, has tremendous potential for human misery, as we have seen.

The term a "thousand years" is used several times in this chapter, and has a special meaning in this context. It does not refer to an exact term of ten centuries, or of nine hundred and ninety-nine years plus one. One thousand is written as one, a unit, followed by zero, zero, zero. Or, one nothing nothing nothing! This indicates an unspecified or unlimited number, but which in fact is nothing! It seems to be part of the nature of humankind that phases and events come in alternating cycles. Therefore, one thousand, as here written, means an unlimited or unspecified term, which may be long or short but is part of a cycle. Thus, we see that the dragon has been chained for just so long a time as we are able to remain in a high consciousness, but he will obtain his release if and when we allow negation to have its way with us.

The experience of Geoffrey, a member of a church I once served, illustrates this principle at work. He owned and operated a fair-sized machine shop closely linked to automobile manufacturing, and he had previously talked with me about his plans to expand his plant. Now he came to see me in great distress. His business of making small parts for the auto industry had been doing well. He had also negotiated a contract with another concern, not related to the auto industry. On the strength of this, he had enlarged his plant and had borrowed heavily to purchase new equipment.

Then two cruel blows descended almost simultaneously. The nation entered a mild recession, causing cutbacks in auto manufacturing, and his regular business was almost nil. But the real catastrophe came when his new contract was rendered valueless. That company had failed and he was left with a zero cash flow and heavily in debt. His lenders had pressed for payment, had foreclosed, and he had lost his business, everything! He was finished; he was wiped out. He was a failure. What should he do now? Should he kill himself? Would I pray for him?

For a few moments I contemplated Geoffrey. He was a picture of despair. I deeply sympathized with him in his predicament. He had suffered a great loss. But possibly my chief reaction was that of a combination of surprise and disappointment, not that these things should have happened to him, but that he should have reacted as he did. It is, of course, a serious matter to lose all one has, in his case upwards of a million dollars, but I could have hoped that with his long exposure to our teachings he would have shown greater resilience.

However, I tried to give him the comfort and counsel he needed. "Geoff," I said, "you've had a terrible blow, but this is not the end. You can make a comeback."

"What with?" he countered. "I've got nothing."

"Now that's not true. You still have the courage and the initiative that enabled you to build your business in the first place. I know your story. Your success was not handed to you on a platter. You built it from scratch and you can do it again. With your experience and know-how you can get a good job anywhere in this city. There are dozens of shops that would be glad to hire you. My suggestion is, forget this reverse. Forget it, and be willing to start over. Take your attention away from what you've lost. They are but transitory material things, anyway. Now focus your attention on the future. Set yourself a new goal. I know you can do it."

This was comfort in the true sense of the word. *Com*, meaning "together" or "with," and *fort*, meaning "fortress, a strong place." To comfort is not to pander to a person's weakness, but to help him discover his latent strength. It took a little time with Geoffrey, but when one is as far down as he was, there is only one way to go, and that is up! We prayed together, and he got a new light in his eye and decided to accept the challenge that this seeming adversity presented. His wife was a fine person, and together they made adjustments in their life-style. He got a job, and when I last heard of him he was on his way up.

For years Geoffrey had been a good Truth student, worked hard, supported the Center, was a good husband, and built a fine business. For "one thousand years" Satan had been bound. Geoffrey had kept his thinking positive and constructive, and all was well with him. Then he fell on hard times (had the "deceiver" and "father of lies" tempted him to be overly ambitious?), and in a flash Satan was free and Geoffrey was assailed by negative, fearful, even suicidal thoughts. But the rider on the white horse, Faithful and True, the Word of God, came to the rescue.

It is well to recognize the presence of such cycles in life. At any stage in our ongoing we are vulnerable to attack. The tendency is for life to assume the characteristics of a roller coaster. However, in a spiritual way we can limit the length of the downs and extend the ups. Recognition that life is a learning process will assist us in overcoming the various challenges. The length of any particular "thousand years" is determined not by the challenge itself, nor by the severity of the problem nor the magnitude of the difficulty, but by the attitude with which it is faced. The Word of God is always available to help us.

John then "saw thrones, and seated on them were those to whom judgment was committed. Also I saw the souls of those who had been beheaded for their testimony to Jesus and for the word of God. . . . They came to life, and reigned with Christ a thousand years. . . . This is the first resurrection. . . . Over such the second death has no power, but they shall be priests of God" (Rev. 20:4-6). Here we have a restatement of the principle of divine justice always at work. "Beheaded for their testimony" means persecuted because of standing for principle. Whatever form the victimization may take, those who make a stand for the principles represented by the Jesus Christ teaching will ultimately be justified. They may have suffered certain material losses (the first death), but they are blessed in being justified (the first resurrection) and shall reign with him a "thousand years," that is, will be vindicated.

But the roller coaster principle again applies, and a cycle ends, for we are told in a passage beginning with verse seven that

Satan will be loosed from his prison. This time he gains support from the four corners of the earth and from Gog and Magog. This indicates that, though apparently we are well along the road of spiritual progress, it is necessary to be constantly vigilant, for negation may assume a totally different guise and threaten our relationship with the indwelling Christ. But "fire came down from heaven and consumed" (Rev. 20:9) the attackers. While not so stated, this is a reminder that once the follower of the Way has made a commitment to the Lamb, he will not be deserted. He is not alone, for the Word of God will come to his rescue as he stands firm in the faith (Rev. 20:7-9).

The verses that follow, from ten to the end of the chapter, have struck terror in the hearts of many who read the Bible literally. The contents appear to condemn miscreants to an eternity of torment. In truth, this symbolizes the cleansing process within the soul of the individual who is consciously and resolutely seeking redemption. In the process of regeneration the soul of the aspirant has been lifted and purified, until it is now seen as one seated on a great white throne. It is this, the purified soul, who consigns the devil to the lake of fire. The "dead, great and small" are standing before the throne, and "the book of life" is opened. The committed soul is able to review his past; thoughts and actions, great and small, important and once seemingly trivial, are judged and seen for what they were in truth—either helpful influences or hindrances. All error is now released. But consignment to the "lake of fire" is not in any way indicative of punishment or retribution. It is a symbol of cleansing and release as we jettison all that is unworthy.

"Then Death and Hades were thrown into the lake of fire" (Rev. 20:14). This signifies letting go of the fear of death and of unnecessary suffering. Not the least of the lessons that we gain from the life and teachings of Jesus Christ is the fact that He likely engineered His own execution in order to demonstrate that the cessation of life in the physical body is not the end. Following His crucifixion, He resurrected, proving that life is continuous. As long as we hold to the erroneous belief in a single lifetime, we will continue to fear death.

We are threefold beings of spirit, soul, and body. Essentially we are spirit; our soul is our constantly changing awareness of ourselves, while our body is the very temporary and impermanent physical housing, given to us for use on this earth plane. Our consciousness can never die. When life leaves our present physical body, our spirit will go to some succeeding plane or planes, the full measure of which we do not yet understand. How good it is to know that: "This that we call death, it is no more than the opening and closing of a door" to another room of life ("The Traveler," James Dillet Freeman). Thus we can joyously be rid of this fear forever. And Hades (standing for unnecessary self-inflicted anguish) also is consigned to the lake of fire when it is seen that there is no point in enduring useless suffering caused by belief in error and negation.

The chapter concludes with the statement, "This is the second death, the lake of fire; and if any one's name was not found written in the book of life, he was thrown into the lake of fire" (Rev. 20:14-15). This helps us understand the earlier reference in verse six, "Blessed and holy is he who shares in the first resurrection! Over such the second death has no power, but they shall be priests of God and of Christ." This means that we shall no longer have any use for the attitudes and emotions that have for so long hindered us in our spiritual progress, but we will be able to cast them aside without a pang, leaving us free of all things that are not of the Christ nature. Again we emphasize, no soul is thrown into the lake of fire—this is symbolic of the growing, unfolding individual casting aside all that is unworthy.

coming down out of heaven from God, prepared as a bride adorned for her husband"
(Rev. 21:2). Metaphysically, this "new Jerusalem," so prepared, stands for spiritual consciousness at its acme of illumination. It is
ready for the complete union with the Christ.
This is confirmed by a great voice from the
throne saying, "Behold, the dwelling of God
is with men. He will dwell with them, and
they shall be his people, and God himself will
be with them" (Rev. 21:3). This is the fulfillment of our seeking, the climax of our search:
conscious union with Source.

As a result of this realization of complete
oneness with God, a new understanding of
the meaning of life will have been achieved.
The truth of what is termed physical death
will be discerned; there will no longer be any
mourning or grief because the belief in physical separation will have been removed. There
will be no sense of bereavement or loss, and
so no need for tears of regret or remorse.
There will be no more pain, because the follower of the Lamb will no longer be doing or
thinking those things that make for unnecessary suffering. The individual will have
an entirely new outlook on life, "for the
former things have passed away" (Rev. 21:4).
A "new heaven" (state of mind) will have pro-

duced a "new earth," a new outlook, and manifest experience.

Then in verse five there is the wonderful promise for all those who may still be on the way, "Behold, I make all things new" (Rev. 21:5). To emphasize the importance of the point that is about to be made, John is instructed to write what follows: "It is done! I am the Alpha and the Omega, the beginning and the end" (Rev. 21:6). This is a repetition of the announcement made in the eighth verse of the first chapter, and the purpose is the same—to underline the necessity for the correct use of "I AM" statements. It means: I AM is all that is necessary. The way in which "I AM" is used is decisive.

Then the promise continues, "To the thirsty I will give from the fountain of the water of life without payment" (Rev. 21:6). Or, to those who thirst enough to overcome negation in consciousness will be given the life-nourishing flow of divine ideas to sustain them through all circumstances. And as they determine to dispense with any tendencies toward cowardice, faithlessness, pollution, murderousness, fornication, sorcery, idolatry, or lying, and throw these negative elements of their characters into the lake of fire, then they, too, will have this heritage.

This is a formidable list of character defects, and one hopes that the follower of the Way will have long since shed these in the literal sense. However, they do serve to underline the necessity for bringing one's thoughts, emotions, and actions into line with the nature of the Lamb.

Assisted by one of the angels who had assisted in the cleansing of consciousness, John is then conducted to a great high mountain from which he is able to see a rapturous vision of the holy city of the new Jerusalem. This is the bride, the wife of the Lamb, or the purged and uplifted consciousness that will achieve the longed-for union with God. Like a rare jewel, it reflects the glory of God. If we include verse seventeen, which refers to one hundred and forty-four cubits (one hundred forty-four being twelve times twelve), the number twelve is referred to twelve times in the verses that comprise the remainder of the chapter. The number twelve stands for wholeness and perfection. It is used throughout the Bible as the number of spiritual completeness and perfection in potential. In this context where the number is used twelve times on "a great, high mountain" (Rev. 21:10), it clearly indicates spiritual completeness and perfection enhanced by some sublime progression beyond our knowing. The meticulous manner of the city's arrangement and the richness of the costly materials employed combine to create the impression of tremendous and precious value. Intuitively, one knows that despite the exalted and laudatory terms used, these are understatements of something that is beyond description. Such is the glory of God!

In this sublime consciousness, the initiate will need no special time nor place for worship, for he will live, move, and have his being in the constant awareness of his oneness with God. For John reports, "I saw no temple in the city, for its temple is the Lord God the Almighty and the Lamb" (Rev. 21:22). In this awareness, all that we think, say, and do will conform with the will and inspiration of God. This will also be our source of light, for "the city has no need of sun or moon to shine upon it, for the glory of God is its light, and its lamp is the Lamb" (Rev. 21:23). "By its light shall the nations walk" (Rev. 21:24) means that, illumined by this intuitive knowing, the initiate will be able to move easily and surely in and through every situation, effectively ruling his emotions and reactions, commanding the respect of all. Even so, this Christ-oriented awareness will never have a closed mind ("its gates shall never be shut" [Rev. 21:25]), but nevertheless will be able immediately to exclude any unworthy concept from entering.

"Through the middle of the street of the city" (Rev. 22:2) flows the river of the water of life, stemming from the throne of God and from the Lamb. This refers to the unceasing flow of divine ideas in God-Mind, which are constantly available to sustain and nourish, easily accessible and unlimited in quantity. From the river of the water of life springs the tree of life that produces twelve kinds of fruit that are our spiritual faculties, or the outpouring of divine ideas. These faculties were discerned by Charles Fillmore to be symbolized for us by Jesus' twelve disciples, who have been represented throughout The Revelation to John as the twenty-four elders (twelve mental powers, but doubled in effect when spiritualized). These are faith, love, judgment, order, strength, power, imagination, understanding, zeal, will, elimination, and life.

The angel continues to describe the illumined condition of those who are continually aware only of the throne of God and of the Lamb by allowing the nature of the Lamb to possess their minds to the exclusion of "anything accursed." If they will keep the nature of the Lamb foremost in their minds ("his name shall be on their foreheads" [Rev. 22:4]), they will enjoy the light of the Lord God "for ever and ever," that is, for as long as they remain in that level of consciousness.

As the angel draws near to the end of his visit with John, he says three times, "I am coming soon" (Rev. 22:7). On the first occasion the statement is prefaced by the same words with which The Revelation to John opens: God sent his angel to show "what must soon take place" (Rev. 22:6). On that occasion, the Comforter had no doubt that the challenges referred to in The Revelation to John would be the lot of the faithful. Now the angel is reminding John that this is still so, but with the added thought, "I am coming soon," or, I am immediately available. This indicates the immediacy of the Holy Spirit to help him. Then as an afterthought, "Blessed is he who keeps the words of the prophecy of this book" (Rev. 22:7).

John fell at the feet of the angel to worship him, but as he had done before as recorded in chapter nineteen, verse ten, the angel brusquely stopped him: "You must not do that! ... Worship God" (Rev. 22:9). This is not only a timely reminder to all to avoid placing teachers and gurus on a pedestal, but also to avoid becoming carried away by worshiping the exaltation of the moment. The follower of the Way is still alive on this earth plane, and he has a responsibility to apply his understanding of the nature of the Lamb in daily life. The admonition to "worship God" is not being fully implemented merely by time being spent in prayer and meditation, but it is necessary to exercise the lamblike qualities of love, compassion, empathy, and forgiveness in one's relationships with suffering humanity.

Now he adopts a curiously philosophical tone: "Let the evildoer still do evil, and the filthy still be filthy, and the righteous still do right, and the holy still be holy. Behold, I am coming soon, bringing my recompense, to repay every one for what he has done" (Rev. 22:11-12). In other words, do not attempt to change the world overnight. People are still people and will behave as people do, for I, God, operating through the law of cause and effect, will be on hand regardless. And he adds the reminder, "I am the Alpha and the Omega" (Rev. 22:13).

Then comes the loving invitation extended in verses fourteen through seventeen: "Blessed are those who wash their robes"

(Rev. 22:14). Anyone who qualifies, by purity of mind and actions, can enter the "new Jerusalem," while those who prefer to remain in the existing worldly state of mind will be excluded until they, too, change.

There follow the two verses, eighteen and nineteen, which would at first appear to intimidate any would-be interpreter from seeking the inner meaning of The Revelation to John. However, this is a metaphysical study and we have realized that the various statements are not to be taken literally, but to be applied in the metaphysical or figurative sense, for this is an examination of human consciousness. We have no more reason to shrink from spiritual understanding of this passage than we have for accepting the literal interpretation of the statement that only 144,000 people will attain salvation, or belief in Armageddon as being some final battle between the forces of good and evil to be fought at some date in the future.

The Revelation to John has consistently followed the law of mind action, teaching that we invariably reap the results of the causes that we have set into motion. We are therefore warned that if we add in our minds to the dread that we may have of the dragon and the beasts and their influence, then the dire effects of the plagues described will be increased in consequence. Also, to the extent that we downplay the regenerative influence of the Lamb, so will the advantages that would otherwise accrue be lessened.

There may now be a temptation to close the book with a sigh, and think, "Well that's that. Jesus Christ made it, and possibly a few others in the intervening centuries have also achieved this exalted state of complete atonement (at-one-ment with the Father). But as for me, I still have a long way to go, and I can leave consideration of these last two chapters until later (a future life perhaps?)." But not so. So timeless is The Revelation to John that even these final chapters have a current lesson for the follower of the Way, whatever his or her position on the spiritual path. Of course, they contain the message of ultimate spiritual atonement, and this is doubtless their primary object. But these closing chapters have an immediacy of application that may not at first have been apparent. This is so particularly when the individual is confronted with an especially difficult challenge.

There are times in the lives of some people when it appears that Truth does not work in their lives. After a long period of praying effectively, of correct use of the mind and imagination, there arises a difficulty of great size. It seems as if the beast is about to be released after "one thousand years" of being chained. Such a one was Rosslyn K., whom I knew as a member of my congregation. She was a sunny, outgoing, healthy, joyous person who practiced the Unity way of life. She was a dedicated, generous, and compassionate individual whom we all felt was bound to live a life of special blessedness. Suddenly, she was stricken with cancer and underwent a colostomy.

As her minister, I asked myself, where had I failed? Where had she failed? Had she harbored secret malignant thoughts? Was there a secret tragedy or disappointment in her life? Anyway, we were all in for another surprise. Her recovery was astonishingly rapid. Her attitude was triumphant and confident; her reactions were completely positive. She remained a happy woman throughout. The experience to her was seemingly no more significant than having a tooth pulled. She had endured what for some can be a crushing experience, but she remained in the consciousness of the "new Jerusalem." After the first shock, she had decided there would be "no more tears, no mourning, nor crying, nor pain, for the former things have passed away."

Why should this have happened to Rosslyn? We decided the challenge was a response to her demand for growth. Of course the law of cause and effect was involved and at some point she must have sown or accepted causes, but the triumphant manner in which she made an overcoming clearly indicated the presence of grace ("Christ is the Lord of Karma," Emmet Fox). It caused me to rethink the message that Unity carries, and to rethink the message contained in The Revelation to John. As we have been faithful in our study of The Revelation to John, and sought to apply the nature of the Lamb to ourselves, we finally reached the last two chapters. We are told the dwelling of God is with us. His love, joy, and peace will be ours. We are told that every tear shall be wiped from our eyes, death will be no more, neither shall there be mourning, crying, nor pain, for the former things have passed away. Behold all things are made new! What a promise of unalloyed bliss, of perfect fulfillment, of uninterrupted joy and harmony. This is the seventh heaven.

Will anyone ever attain this on this plane? Is this what life is all about? Unity appears to teach this. Superficially, we appear to be teaching that if the individual follows the Christ way, thinks positively, behaves lovingly, speaks helpfully, tithes generously, and lives compassionately, then all will be well; there will be no more pain, no challenges, no sickness, no sorrow, no poverty—only complete well-being, harmony in all relationships, radiant health, adequate supply; in fact, continuous happiness!

No! I do not believe that this is what Unity teaches, nor do I believe that this is the message of the last chapters of The Revelation to John. It is close, but there is a subtle and important difference. Unity does teach fulfillment, happiness, and well-being, and the symbolism of John's revelation does promise these—but not necessarily in the physical and material framework that we are prone to associate with fulfillment, happiness, and well-being. The biblical message is that we find fulfillment, however defined, as we find God; that is, we come into the realization of our essential oneness with God.

If we are honest with ourselves, we will probably find that our happiest and most fulfilling moments were not when we achieved or possessed some long sought after desire, but when we were in the process of striving or working toward that goal. Many couples, who by this time have their homes, have raised and educated their families, and are happy, can look back on the deeply satisfying times when they were building a home on a slender income. The rich times of their lives were when they were striving, reaching, facing, and overcoming difficulties, and drawing on their inner resources, that is, consciously or unconsciously seeking God. This is in truth what life is all about, for we are truly problem-solving entities, but above all, we are spiritual entities. Naturally, we deeply enjoy our achievements and possessions and the satisfaction of attainment, but these feelings are not lasting. We conquer one peak, and scarcely have we caught our breath before there appears another mountain to climb.

So humankind progresses spiritually and looks forward to perfect fulfillment, but that fulfillment is not so much found in perfect mastery over all the events of life as it is in mastery over one's reactions to those events. Thus it would appear that we reach our perfect state not when we have no problems, but when we can joyously and triumphantly overcome everything that life can ever present to us; in other words, complete mastery over our own reactions in the realization that we are one with God, good.

So the joyous message of *Revelation: The Road to Overcoming* is that as we follow the teaching of Jesus Christ, we must and will overcome all that is ever presented to us. The heart of the Christian message is not that we will always find it easy and soft, but that as we actively seek to know God, we will be able to handle the challenges of life. Uneventful harmony sounds very attractive, but it does not produce growth, and our purpose in living, whether on this or some future plane, is to grow! The very worst way to meet any challenge, whether financial, of human relationships, or health, is to resist and allow it to make us unhappy. The way of The Revelation to John is to be nonresistant and become as the Lamb. Rejoice and know that you can overcome as you are faithful and true, for God is there to help.

The message of The Revelation to John, briefly restated, is: follow the teachings of Jesus Christ; cultivate the nature of the Lamb; fearlessly face the error in your own thinking; deal courageously with your shortcomings; be loving and inoffensive to others; recognize that all seeming evil is the product of your own misguided beliefs and actions; get rid of grudges and resentments about the past; have faith and hope in the face of trial; and know that with the help of God in prayer you can and will overcome. "The grace of the Lord Jesus be with all the saints. Amen" (Rev. 22:21). In this, the consciousness of the indwelling Christ, survival is assured.

ABOUT THE AUTHOR

Charles A. Neal was born in London, England, where he was deputy head of the Speakers Department of the Conservative Party central office when Winston Churchill was chairman of the party. He came to the United States in 1945.

He is a longtime Unity minister and has served Unity churches in Colorado Springs, Colorado; Atlanta, Georgia; Detroit, Michigan; St. Petersburg and Miami, Florida; and, most recently, Tulsa, Oklahoma.

As vice president of the Unity Ministers Association, he was elected the first president of the Association of Unity Churches in 1965 and was appointed director of ministry services of the Association in 1981. He was awarded an honorary doctorate by the Association and was the 1998 recipient of the Association's Light of God Expressing award.

He has contributed numerous articles to *Unity Magazine.* He is married to Nancy Neal, herself an ordained Unity minister and a past president of the Association. Nancy Neal is also a onetime director of what is now called the Silent Unity Telephone Prayer Ministry.

Printed in the U.S.A.   149-1850-5M-12-99